Access 2000
An Introductory Course for Students

Titles in this series

This is one of a series of course books for students, covering the three major components of the Microsoft Office 2000 suite of software.

Access 2000
An Introductory Course for Students
Sue Coles and Jenny Rowley
ISBN 1 903300 14 2

Access 2000
An Advanced Course for Students
Sue Coles and Jenny Rowley
ISBN 1 903300 15 0

Excel 2000
An Introductory Course for Students
Jim Muir
ISBN 1 903300 16 9

Excel 2000
An Advanced Course for Students
Jim Muir
ISBN 1 903300 17 7

Word 2000
An Introductory Course for Students
Sue Coles and Jenny Rowley
ISBN 1 903300 18 5

Word 2000
An Advanced Course for Students
Sue Coles and Jenny Rowley
ISBN 1 903300 19 3

To order, please contact our distributors:
Plymbridge Distributors, Estover Road, Plymouth, PL6 7PY.
Tel: 01752 202301 Fax: 01752 202333 Email: orders@plymbridge.com

Access 2000
An Introductory
Course for Students

Sue Coles
Department of Business and Management Studies
Crewe and Alsager Faculty
Manchester Metropolitan University

Jenny Rowley
School of Management and Social Sciences
Edge Hill College of Higher Education

m
Learning Matters

Acknowledgements

Windows 98™ and Word™ © Microsoft Corporation, all rights reserved. Screen displays from Word 2000 and Windows 98 reprinted with permission from Microsoft Corporation.

First published in 2001 by Learning Matters Ltd.

British Library Cataloguing in Publication Data

A CIP record for this book is available from the British Library.

ISBN 1 903300 14 2

Cover and text design by Code 5 Design Associates Ltd
Project management by Deer Park Productions
Typeset by PDQ Typesetting
Printed and bound in Great Britain

Learning Matters Ltd
58 Wonford Road
Exeter EX2 4LQ
Telephone 01392 215560
Email: info@learningmatters.co.uk
www.learningmatters.co.uk

Contents

Topic 1   Working with this book   1

Topic 2   Working with Access 2000   6

Topic 3   Creating a simple Access database table   10

Topic 4   Creating further tables   16

Topic 5   Creating and changing data   22

Topic 6   Amending data   27

Topic 7   Changing and reorganising data   32

Topic 8   Basic queries   37

Topic 9   More simple queries   44

Topic 10   More advanced queries   49

Topic 11   Screen forms   54

Topic 12   Reports   60

Topic 13   Mailing reports and queries   66

Topic 14   More on forms   71

Topic 15   More on reports   78

Topic 16   Relational databases   83

Topic 17   Forms, queries and reports in relational databases   88

Topic 18   Making improvements   92

Topic 19   Switchboard forms   97

Appendix 1   Data   101

Appendix 2   Portfolio items checklist   104

Index   108

v

Features in the text

The following features have been used throughout the book to make the practical instructions clear:

1. Bold capitals indicate a feature from the screen, for example **BUTTON** or **DIALOG BOX NAME**.
   Menu instructions are also presented this way: **EDIT-COPY** means choose **COPY** from the **EDIT** menu.

2. White bold capitals in a panel indicate the names of keys on the keyboard, for example **ESC** or **F1**.

3. Bold text in upper and lower case indicates names of **Fields**, **Tables**, **Queries**, **Forms** and **Reports**.

4. Italic text on a shaded background indicates *Text to be keyed in*.

Working with this book

Topic objectives

This topic introduces you to this book, and the ways in which it will help you to learn about Access 2000 and how to manage data using a database. The topic shows you how to:

- work through the exercises in this book to complete an assignment or assessment
- understand the way in which Access 2000 manages data.

Approach

This book introduces you to Access 2000, Microsoft's widely used database software, using a step-by-step approach. It includes many exercises that offer the opportunity to practise and develop data handling skills.

Access is a component of the Office 2000 suite of application software, which also includes Word, Excel and PowerPoint. Word is a powerful word processor suitable for producing a wide variety of documents. Excel is a spreadsheet package that is useful for numerical and financial applications. PowerPoint is a presentation package that supports the creation of printed and electronic slides and slideshows. Documents, data and objects can be easily transferred between these different applications.

This book is designed for anyone who wants to learn how to use Access. This includes students in further and higher education, and professional users who need to use a database to manage data. Students who might benefit from this book are likely to be studying databases as part of an ICT skills programme, and may be on any one of a number of courses. For students on information systems, information management, business studies, management studies, and marketing courses the skills outlined in this book should be viewed as essential for the completion of their studies, and for their continuing professional life.

The underlying philosophy of this book is concerned with learning by doing. The unique and popular feature of the book is the focus on activities and exercises. Each topic gives you a number of exercises to complete. In each topic, the relevance and function of the new concepts are explained, and detailed instructions are given on how to carry out the exercises. As you work through the book you will gradually build up a database relating to Halwyn Video Store a fictitious business somewhere in Cornwall. Later exercises rely on tables of data built up in earlier exercises, so it is advisable to approach the topics in order.

You are encouraged to save the databases that you create, as you work through this book, in a special folder or directory. This folder will include the portfolio of your work. Tutors can select from the exercises in this book and define a set of exercises to be completed for an assignment. The final topic in this book covers ways in which the databases created can be organised for presentation to a tutor so that work can be submitted either in print form or electronically to satisfy the requirements of an assignment.

The book can be used as a basis for independent study or as the basis for class activities. In either context it is important to:

- Work methodologically through the exercises in the order in which they are presented; data entered in tables in earlier exercises is required for queries, forms and reports in later exercises.
- Take time for rest and reflection and break learning into manageable sessions.
- Think about what you are doing!
- Expect to make mistakes; think about the consequences of mistakes and learn from them. If you never make a mistake you will not learn as much from this book as someone who has had to experiment and deviate from the instructions.
- Remember that this book hasn't got all the answers. It is selective. Continue learning by experimentation, and by using help and other guides after you have mastered the content of this book.

Creating your Access 2000 database

This task shows you how to create a database file, which will hold all the components of a database that you will create in working through this book. To create and save your first blank database:

1 Either start Access by clicking on the **START** button in the taskbar, selecting **PROGRAMS** and selecting **MICROSOFT ACCESS**, or if you have a shortcut icon on your desktop for Access then you may double-click on it to start Access.

2 Choose the **CREATE A NEW DATABASE USING BLANK DATABASE** option. If Access is already running then choose **FILE-NEW** and double-click on the **BLANK DATABASE** icon.

3 The **FILE NEW DATABASE** dialog box will be displayed.

4 In the **FILE NAME** box give the database the filename *Halwyn Videos*. Click on the **CREATE** button.

5 A blank database is created and saved in your My Documents folder. Close Access using the **FILE-EXIT** command.

Note: You may save your database file in an alternative folder, particularly if you are working on a networked computer.

What is a database?

A database is a structured collection of related data. The concept of a database does not only apply to data held in electronic formats; your address book would be an example of a paper-based database. However, data is most commonly held in an electronic format, and it is electronic databases that are the theme of this book.

All organisations collect data which they store in databases. For example, a database could be used keep records of the transactions that they perform with suppliers and customers. Large database applications have been common in industry for many years. Databases of component parts are important in production and maintenance applications in the engineering industry. Service based industries, such as the health service or the banking industry, are particularly interested in databases of customers or clients. Each department or function within a business maintains a database that supports its specific activities. Thus finance departments have large databases that allow them to record the financial transactions that have been undertaken in the business, ranging from payment of salaries to sales and purchases. Marketing departments will maintain databases that show sales orders placed, the performance of specific sales staff and customer profiles.

When databases were first widely used they tended to be largely text and number based. Now images, pictures, video clips and sound may be embedded in multimedia database applications. Databases can be accessed over the Internet, so, for example, a customer could find out details about a particular product and that product information could be available in a variety of multimedia formats.

Typically, a database holds data in the form of records. Each record relates to one transaction (e.g. a sales order) or one item or individual (e.g. a patient). Any specific database has a standard record format, and the same details are stored in each record. So, for example, if the database stores the name, address, age and sex of one customer, it will generally store the same data for each other customer whose details have been entered on the database.

3

Why use a database?

There is no point in storing data unless you want to do something with it. So a library will store data about loan materials, items out on loan and borrowers so that it can function properly. A library would be unlikely to be interested in their borrowers' weekly shop at a supermarket as that data would not be relevant to their operation. On the other hand, the supermarket would be interested in what customers buy so that they can stock the right amount of products.

Databases are not only very good at storing data, they are also very good at manipulating it. Records in a database can be sorted into any order. Sets of records can be extracted – for example, sales records over a certain time period. Items in records can be totalled, for example, to find total monthly sales and totals can be grouped so total sales by region can be calculated.

Thinking about storing data

1 At present the owner of Halwyn Videos has a book in which he records details about the video cassettes he has for rental. This is a separate book from the one he uses to record which videos are out on loan. Imagine you are the owner and you have just bought a new set of videos. What would you want to note down about them?

2 Design a membership application form for Halwyn Bay Videos, either on paper or using a word processor. Think carefully about what details you want about prospective members.

3 If you were considering the data needed for a dental patient's record card, how would this differ from the personal details required by the video rental business?

The Access 2000 database management system

Access is a database management system (DBMS) that provides a means of storing and managing data. There are four main components of an Access database that we will be considering in this book. These are:

- tables
- queries
- forms
- reports.

Tables

Like all database management systems, Access stores data as a set of records. Records are held in a table, which organises the data by rows and columns. The minimum requirement for a database is that you have at least one table. Advanced databases will have many tables that are linked but at this introductory level will we concentrate on single tables of data.

Each row is a record and it contains the collection of specific details for that record. Each column in a table represents a specific detail, such as a patient's National Health number or the date an employee commenced their employment.

Queries

As mentioned previously, a database is created with a purpose in mind. That purpose involves asking questions, or queries, for example, 'Which members have a video that is overdue?' 'What is the date of Mr Brown's next appointment?' Queries are used to select records from a database to answer such questions.

Forms

Data presented, particularly on-screen, in the form of a table may not always be easy to read. If the records are long then you may have to scroll across the screen in order to be able to see all the data and you won't be able to see it all at the same time.

Screen forms are particularly useful to customise the way in which the data from records in tables or queries are displayed on screen. Their main purpose is to provide a user-friendly interface for the entry of new records or for editing existing records. There are wizards to help you create screen forms or you can create your own design from scratch so that the data is presented just the way you want it.

Forms allow text and labels to be added to give instructions to the person entering the data and clarify any options, such as '1 = Adult, 2 = Child, 3 = Concessionary'. A full range of fonts and colours can be used in forms as well as the choice of pre-set backgrounds. Lines, rectangles and logos can be added to give the form a pleasing appearance.

Reports

Although data can be printed from tables, queries and forms, historically data could only be printed using a 'report' layout. This feature is retained by modern databases as a report design can include headers and footers, and can calculate sub-totals and grand totals. As with forms, font, colours, lines, boxes and logos can be incorporated to make a professional looking printout.

A report can be used to print data from tables or queries, and a selected set of details from either the table or query may be chosen so that just the relevant data is selected for the printout.

Presenting your work for assessment purposes

As you work through this book you will create a number of the database objects described above. These objects (tables, queries, forms, and reports) work together to form your database application.

As you build the database application you can submit it for assessment at the end of each topic. Sometimes the evidence you submit will be electronic, sometimes it will be printouts and in some topics there will be a mixture of the two.

If you are submitting work electronically, your assessor may ask you to e-mail it to them as an attachment to an e-mail message. As you create new objects, and particularly if these involve on-screen display (for example, table datasheets and forms) or printouts (all objects), you should think about developing a personal style in your choice of fonts and colour. Do not get too carried away – the best styles rarely use more than two fonts.

To help you keep track of your progress you will find a portfolio checklist in Appendix 2.

Working with Access 2000

Topic objectives

This topic introduces you to the windows you will use when using Access and covers more basics concerning the setting up of a database. The topic shows you how to:

- open a database
- become familiar with the Access and Database windows
- understand more about records and fields and the planning required to set up a database
- find help and use the Office Assistant.

Opening a database

In the last topic a blank database file **Halwyn Videos** was created. Although we have not created a table as yet, the database file exists. Here we open it so that you can familiarise yourself with the Access and Database windows.

1. To open the database, start Access (if it is not running) as described in the previous topic. Select the file **Halwyn Videos** from the list in the **OPEN AN EXISTING DATABASE** section.

2. If the file is not listed, this may be because it has not been created – refer back to Topic 1. Alternatively, choose Open an existing file. In the **OPEN DATABASE** dialog box select the **Access Databases** folder. Select the file **Halwyn Videos** from the list below the **LOOK IN** box. Click on **OPEN**.

The Access window

Your screen should resemble that in Figure 2.1. The Access window is the larger window and we shall consider this first before looking at the smaller window, the Database window. The Access window has the following components:

- **Title bar** – shows that you are in Microsoft Access.
- **Access control menu** – in the very top left-hand corner (key icon). Window control buttons are at the right of the title bar. These may be Minimise, Maximise and Close or Minimise, Restore and Close depending on whether you have Access open as full screen or not. If Access is not full screen, click on the Maximise button to make the window full screen.
- **Access main menu** – showing the menus, File, Edit, View, Insert, Tools, Window and Help. This menu layout has much in common with other Microsoft Office applications such as Word.
- **Toolbar** – most of the toolbar buttons are shortcuts to commands that can be issued using the menus. Notice that many of the buttons are 'greyed out' or inactive

(nothing happens if you click on them), as with a blank database there are not many commands which will do anything useful. As you build and work with the database then more commands are applicable and their buttons will become active.

- **Status bar** – at the bottom of the screen. Indicates status, e.g. 'Ready'

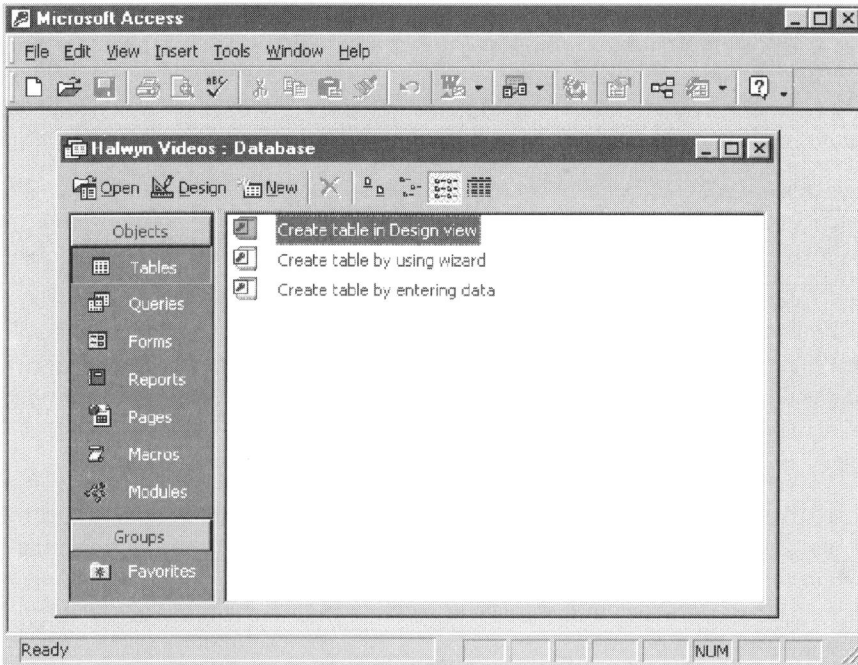

FIGURE 2.1

The Database window

This window allows you to create or access any object (table, query, form, report, etc.) in the database by clicking on one of the object types listed at the left-hand side of the window. In a blank database such as this, the **TABLES** object is selected as a database must have a minimum of one table so a table must be the first thing to be created.

The Database window has its own title bar and menu/tool bar:

- **Title bar** – shows that you have opened the **Halwyn Videos** database.
- **Menu/tool bar** – commands for working with tables are available on this bar. As you create different objects you will see that the commands on this menu/tool bar are specific to the database object (table, query, form or report) that you are working with.
- **Object list** – the large space on the right of the window is to list the names of all the objects, in this case tables, that you might create in the database. At the moment it is empty apart from three commands that can be used to create a table.

Planning a database

Databases are created to serve a purpose and that often involves solving problems – for example, 'Does the video store have a particular video in stock or are they all out on loan?' If a database is to be useful then it needs to able to answer the kinds of questions posed by problems that are likely to arise. Thought needs to be given to the range of problems that might occur in a situation and the data needed to provide the answers. Access allows you to redesign tables, so if you discover later that additional data is required then the database can be modified so that this data can be recorded.

For small databases concerned with small problems, the task of planning the database is relatively straightforward. However, be aware that large databases dealing with complex problems require detailed and often lengthy planning. Often many people are involved in their design. For example, a database system may be used by a hospital or in a college/university administration system.

In this book we shall be considering the database needs of a small video rental business, focusing on the data recorded about the video stock held and borrowers.

In a video rental business, data concerning other aspects of the business could be recorded, such as details of videos on loan or hire rates for different categories or formats of media. In Access, this data could be recorded as additional tables in the database that could be linked together. However, this is beyond the scope of this book and you should proceed to the companion book, *Access 2000 An Advanced Course for Students*, to learn more when you have completed this book.

Tables

A table generally holds data about one type of thing, for example, videos or patients. There are usually lots of this particular thing – perhaps, tens or hundreds of different videos depending on the size of the business. A table of data about borrowers would hold details about each borrower.

Records and fields

A collection of details about an individual video is known as a *record*. For each video there is a separate record in the table. Each record is composed of data about the video, such as, title, category, censor rating and so on. Each item of data within the record is known as a *field*.

Before data can be entered into the database, each field in a record needs to be defined. Each field needs a name and some information regarding the type of data it is intended to hold. For example, if the database knows that the field is a date then it could use it for calculation, to work out someone's age perhaps.

Fields should be given names to describe the kind of data they will eventually hold, e.g. date of purchase. It is important to distinguish between the name of a field and the data which that field contains. For example, the field named **Date of Purchase** will hold dates. The field names can be considered to be the column headings in the table and each row in the table is a separate record. Therefore, each record in the table will have fields with the same name but containing different data.

In an Access database it is important that each record is different from every other record so that it can be selected without confusion. The video store may have more than one copy of *Chicken Run* so an identifying field such as a video ID number is often created to make it easier to make each record unique. This field can be used as a unique identifier and is called a primary key. A *primary key* is a field that uniquely identifies a record.

Field names

1 Consider creating a database of food items in a supermarket.

2 Make a list of data required and give each data item a suitable field name, for example, the selling price of the item would have the field name **Selling Price**.

The Office Assistant

In common with all Microsoft Office applications, the Office Assistant will appear to guide you. The Office Assistant is an animated graphic that floats over your work, and if your PC has a sound card, it also attracts your attention through sound. Clicking on the Office Assistant button in the toolbar will display the Office Assistant if it is hidden. To hide the Office Assistant, right-click on it and choose **HIDE**.

1 Display the Office Assistant if it is not visible and click on it.

2 Enter the question 'How do I create a table?' into the box at the bottom of the speech balloon, replacing the text **Type your question here, and click search**.

3 Click on the **SEARCH** button. Choose the **CREATE A TABLE** option.

4 A Help window appears and you can follow the appropriate link. Choose **CREATE A TABLE FROM SCRATCH** then choose **SEE EXAMPLES OF WHAT TABLES ARE AND HOW THEY WORK**.

5 Click the graphic and read pages 1 and 2 of the information presented. As you can see, there are many links you could follow to help you answer the question, but for now we will exit Help.

6 Click on the **CLOSE** button of this Help window and the **CLOSE** button of the original Help window to return to the Access and Database window.

7 If you wish to close Access choose **FILE-EXIT**.

9

Other routes to help

There are four other routes find to help information:

▪ Pull down the **HELP** menu and select **MICROSOFT ACCESS HELP**, and the Office Assistant will appear. You can also hide the Office Assistant using this menu.

▪ Press the function key **F1** to cause the Office Assistant to appear.

▪ Pull down the **HELP** menu and select **WHAT'S THIS** or press **SHIFT+F1** The pointer changes to an arrow and question mark that can be used to point to anything. Clicking on that object will display a small box with additional information if it is available. To remove the question mark and return to the normal pointer press **ESC**.

▪ In most dialog boxes in the title bar there is a help button that has a question mark on it. Click on this and then click on the part of the dialog box that you want to know more about.

Creating a simple Access database table

Topic objectives

We are now ready to design the first table in the Halwyn Videos database. This topic shows you how to:

- create a table using a variety of methods
- understand the design and datasheet views of tables
- define the type of data to be stored in the database.

We shall explore the different methods of creating a table so that you can find out what each of the options presented in the Database window does. Each method is slightly different but the end result is the same. Hence, we will be creating the same table three times and will be discarding two of these at the end of this topic.

🔲	Create table in Design view
🔲	Create table by using wizard
🔲	Create table by entering data

Creating the *Video* table

The first set of data that we will store will be a list of videos held by the rental business. Before any data can be entered into the database, a table to store the data needs to be designed. This means specifying the fields that will make up the records in the **Video** table and defining the type of data that will be stored in those fields.

The next stage in the construction of the database is to design and create the table that holds the details of the video stock of the business. There are three methods of creating a table, which are listed as commands in the database window. These are **CREATE TABLE IN DESIGN VIEW, CREATE TABLE BY USING WIZARD** or **CREATE TABLE BY ENTERING DATA**. We shall look at the three ways to create a very simple table.

Create table by using Wizard

1 Open the **Halwyn Videos** database.

2 Double-click on **CREATE TABLE BY USING WIZARD**. Under **SAMPLE TABLES** in the **Business** category, select **PRODUCTS**. This is the nearest type of table to the one required.

3 You can now choose suitable fields from the **SAMPLE FIELDS** section. At this stage we are concerned with naming the fields in the database *not* entering data. A field in which a serial number can later be stored would be a good way to uniquely identify each video. Access does this for you using 'ID' fields, in this case a field called **ProductID**. So under **Sample fields** select **PRODUCTID** and click on ▸ to add this field to the **Fields in my new table** list.

4 A more appropriate name for the **ProductID** field would be **Video ID**. Click on the **RENAME FIELD** button and enter the name *VideoID*. Click **OK**.

5 To keep this table very simple we will add one more field, the title of the video. In the **Sample fields** list, **PRODUCTNAME** is the nearest equivalent. Add this to the **Fields in my new table** list and rename it as *Title*.

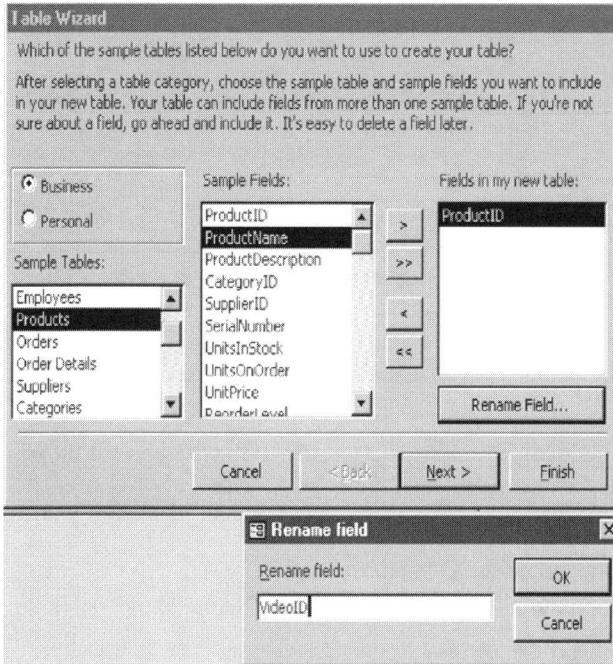

FIGURE 3.1

6 Click on **NEXT>** and give your table the name *Video1*. You should give your table a name that refers to the item about which it is storing data. Note that the option to allow the Wizard to set a primary key is set to **Yes** – do not change this. The Wizard will make the **VideoID** into a primary key field, as we shall see later.

7 Click on **FINISH**. The table displays ready for you to enter data. Enter just two records as shown. Note that you cannot enter anything into the **VideoID** field, this is because Access is taking care of the serial numbers and adding them in automatically. If the **Title** column is not wide enough you can widen it by pointing to the right side of the grey heading box (the pointer should change shape to a vertical line and horizontal double-headed arrow) and dragging.

FIGURE 3.2

8 Click on the **CLOSE** button. If you have altered the column width, Access will ask you if you want to save the layout changes. Click on **YES**. You should now see Video1 listed in the Database window.

11

Create table by entering data

Another way to create a table is by entering data directly. This is the opposite approach to the previous method. Access provides default field names, **Field1**, **Field2**, etc., that you can rename at a later stage.

1 Double-click on **CREATE TABLE BY ENTERING DATA**. A blank table appears. Enter the same data as before.

FIGURE 3.3

Table2 : Table			
Field1	Field2	Field3	Fi
The Perfect Storm			
▶ X-Men			

2 Click on the **CLOSE** button of this table window. Access asks if you want to save the table say **YES**; give the table the name ***Video2*** and click on **OK**. Access then warns that there is no primary key, so say **YES** to ask for one to be created automatically. You should now have two tables listed in the Database window.

Note: This method does not allow you to alter the field names until you switch to design view (see Design view and Datasheet view below).

Create a new table in Design view

Finally, we shall create a table using the **Table Design Window**.

1 Double click on **CREATE A NEW TABLE IN DESIGN VIEW**. In the **Field Name** column enter the name ***VideoID***. Open the **DATA TYPE** drop-down list and choose **AUTONUMBER**. Data types are discussed in the following section.

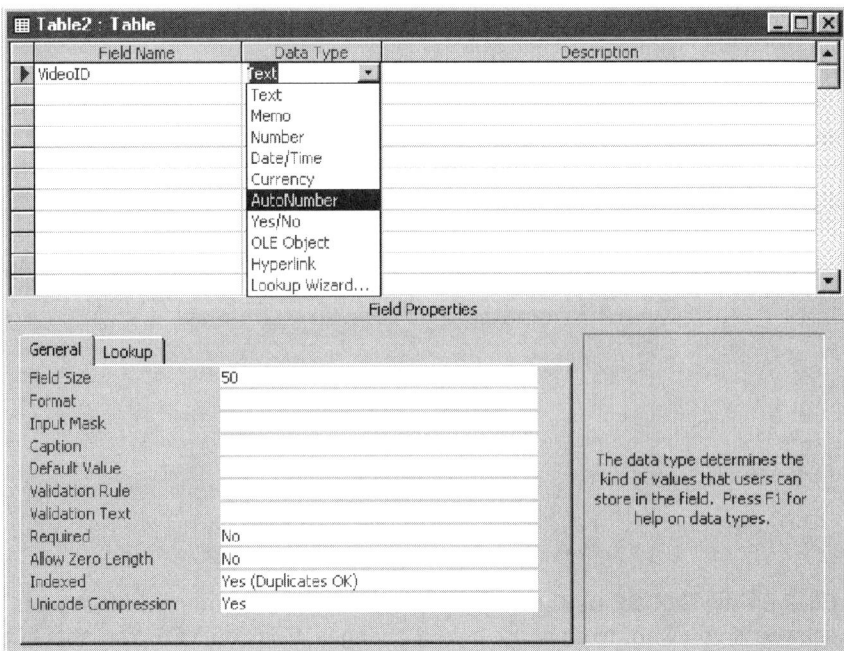

FIGURE 3.4

Table2 : Table			_ □ X
Field Name	Data Type	Description	
▶ VideoID	Text		
	Text		
	Memo		
	Number		
	Date/Time		
	Currency		
	AutoNumber		
	Yes/No		
	OLE Object		
	Hyperlink		
	Lookup Wizard...		

Field Properties

General	Lookup
Field Size	50
Format	
Input Mask	
Caption	
Default Value	
Validation Rule	
Validation Text	
Required	No
Allow Zero Length	No
Indexed	Yes (Duplicates OK)
Unicode Compression	Yes

The data type determines the kind of values that users can store in the field. Press F1 for help on data types.

2 In the next row, enter the field name *Title*. The default data type is Text so it is not necessary to set this. Click back in the **VideoID** row and click the **PRIMARY KEY** button 🔑 to set this as the field that uniquely identifies each record.

3 Click on the **SAVE** button 💾 and give this table the name *Video3*. Close the **Table Design Window**.

We now have three tables that are essentially the same. The first two methods involved entering some data (but note that it is not necessary to enter it all when a table is first created), whereas the third did not. Often tables need to be modified after they have been created and this has to be done using the **Table Design Window**. It is for this reason that the authors prefer this method, and any further table creation or modification will be done using the **Table Design Window**.

Design view and Datasheet view

Tables can be viewed in two ways, either so that you can see the data that they contain (Datasheet view) or so you can see their design (Design view).

1 Select the table **Video1** in the **Database Window**. Click on the **OPEN** button 📂 to open the table in datasheet view and inspect the data. Close the table. Open **Video2** in datasheet view, inspect it, close it and finally look at the data in the **Video3** table. You should notice that in **Video2** the field names are different – **ID** and **Field1**, which do not indicate the kind of data they will store.

2 Now look at each table in turn again but this time open the design view by clicking on the **DESIGN** button 📐. The only difference is the names of the fields in **Video2**.

3 Open **Video2** in design view. Replace the field names **ID** with *VideoID* and **Field1** with *Title*. Save the changes and close the table. Review all three tables in design view again they should all be the same. Close all the tables

The three methods of creating a table have resulted in the same design, so it is a matter of personal preference which one you use when creating your own databases.

Deleting and renaming tables

There is no need for three tables so we shall delete two of them and rename the one left.

1 Check all tables are closed. Select **Video2** and press the **DELETE** key. Access asks you to confirm the delete operation. Repeat this to delete table **Video3**.

2 Select **Video1** and choose **EDIT-RENAME** and remove the **1** so that this table is now called **Video**.

13

Data types

Every field in a table must have its data type defined. Most data is 'alphanumeric' – i.e. text and numbers (in fact, all characters) in a text format, so Access sets the default data type as text. That is, if you don't assign a data type to a field it will automatically be in text format.

There is a variety of other data types, such as number, date, currency and yes/no. It is important to select the appropriate data type for each field. Use number and currency when you are storing data that you might want to handle in a mathematical way, e.g. total it. Numbers that are not intended to be manipulated mathematically should be defined as text – for example, phone numbers, student numbers or other numerical codes. Often these numbers have 'leading zeros', so that the student number 00987654 would lose the first two zeros if the data type was defined as numeric resulting, in 987654.

The following data types are available in Access:

- **Text:** Suitable for text and non-mathematical number. Unless you specify otherwise, Access will make a text field 50 alphanumeric characters long – that is you can enter data (letters and numbers) up to this length. Examples include names, titles and addresses.
- **Number:** Suitable for data on which you intend to perform mathematical calculations. If the data is a price or cost then use the currency data type. An example is a student grade.
- **Currency:** Suitable for money values. It is not recommend to use the **Number** data type for currency values because numbers to the right of the decimal may be rounded during calculations. The **Currency** data type maintains a fixed number of digits to the right of the decimal. Examples include rental fee or dental plan contribution.
- **AutoNumber:** Microsoft Access inserts a number automatically into this type of field. The number it inserts is the next number in an ascending series starting at 1 and stepping up by 1. This makes a good primary key field as each number is unique for each record. However, as a consequence you cannot edit this number and if you later delete a record that number is 'lost'. This data type is used primarily to give uniqueness to each record. Examples include a video ID number or a patient number.
- **Date/Time:** Suitable for storing dates and times. A variety of display formats are available, or you can create your own. An example is date of registration.
- **Yes/No:** Suitable for data that can have only one of two values, i.e. Yes/No, True/False, On/Off. Examples include has full driving licence, wears dentures.
- **Memo:** Suitable for storing textual data longer than 255 characters, which is the maximum available in a text field. A **Memo** field can contain up to 32,000 characters. An example is a patient's medical notes.

Primary key

In a relational database it is important to have records that are unique from one another. This means that the data stored in one field (or possibly a combination of fields) must be unique in every record. This field can then be nominated as the primary key and Access will check that each record has different data in its primary key field(s).

If a simple database application is required where there is only one table, then it may not be important that each record is unique and in this case you would tell Access not to set a primary key. However, the setting of a primary key is highly recommended. It not only speeds data retrieval but also enables you to add other tables to the database that can be linked to the existing one.

Modifying a table design

At present our table only contains two fields and two records. Before we add any more data we need to consider what other data concerning a video cassette we need.

1 Select the table **Video** in the **Database Window** and open it in design view. Add the following fields (the corresponding data will be added in Topic 5).

VideoID	AutoNumber
Title	Text
Video Category	Text
Censor Rating	Text
Date of Acquisition	Date/Time
Format	Yes/No
Cost	Currency

FIGURE 3.5

2 Your database design should look like the screen shot below. Save and close the table.

15

Video : Table

Field Name	Data Type
VideoID	AutoNumber
Title	Text
Video Category	Text
Censor Rating	Text
Date of Acquisition	Date/Time
Format	Yes/No
Cost	Currency

FIGURE 3.6

We have added quite a few more fields. So why do we need these extra fields? After all, it will mean typing in a lot more data. The video category (horror, comedy, etc.) and format (VHS, DVD) can help a customer to find a suitable film.

The date of acquisition will tell the company how long it has owned the video. When it is time to sell it off, if the cost price is known then a markdown could be calculated. The censor rating will enable a check on the suitability of the borrower so that we do not lend an 18 rating to an under-age borrower.

Portfolio item

Halwyn Videos – **Video** table with 7 fields and 2 records.

Creating further tables

Topic objectives

This topic offers you further practice on:

- designing tables
- defining field properties.

It also shows you how to:

- print a table definition.

Creating your own database

In the last two topics you created the **Halwyn Videos** database, and put one table in the database, **Video**. Most database applications comprise several tables. These are linked together into a relational database as discussed in Topic 16. This topic asks you to create a second table, **Customer**, as part of the **Halwyn Videos** databases. Full instructions are not given, as the topic is designed to encourage you to reflect on your learning in Topic 3 and to assess whether you understand some of the basic ideas about the structure and definition of databases. These ideas are important even if you never expect to define a database in your life (after this one!), because an appreciation of database structures helps you to understand the use of databases. You will use databases in leisure, home, study and work activities.

Some of the later exercises in this book use the **Customer** table. This is a less standardised table than **Video**. Since you do not have full instructions on the definition of the table there may be some variations between the outcomes that you achieve with this table in later exercises and those shown in the book. This is a deliberate ploy. It means that you will have to think things through for yourself. There are more likely to be difficulties and problems that you will need to resolve than when working with the **Video** table. Accordingly, exercises on the **Customer** table are normally only introduced after concepts have been introduced and practised using the **Video** table.

The **Customer** table is introduced to encourage additional practice, but it also has another purpose. The **Customer** table is an additional table in the **Halwyn Videos** database. Most databases comprise several tables. The **Video** table is useful in identifying the video stock, but if we want to record any transactions associated with the videos, such as order and purchase, or loans to customers, then it is necessary to create other tables. For example, to keep a record of which video is on loan to which customer, it is necessary to develop a customer table, so that we know the identity of our customers. We also need a mechanism for linking individual videos to customers, when a customer has specific videos on loan. This can be achieved through a further table called the loans table. We return to these ideas and explore the concept of a relational database further in Topic 16. For now, it is sufficient to understand that the **Customer** table forms part of the **Halwyn Videos** database.

Designing the *Customer* table

In this topic you are asked to create your own table, called **Customer**. Your task is to decide how to define the table, in terms of the fields to include, the data type for each field and any field properties, such as field length or date format. Your table must be appropriate for the specification described below, and, in the interests of working through later exercises in this book, it must include one or two basic features as indicated below:

Specification

The purpose of the **Customer** table is to hold a simple but effective list of the customers of Halwyn Videos. This is a registration database that allows Halwyn videos to maintain a list of their customers. Main uses of the database are likely to be to mail promotional literature, relating, for example, to new releases or special offers, and to follow up any videos that are not returned within the loan period. Information in the database could also be used as a security check to ensure that individuals tendering cards in store are the registered cardholders. Reports from the database might be created to provide management information on the customer profile, possibly in terms of age, interests, and the geographical location and spread of customers.

Your **Customer** table should exhibit the following features:

1. At least three different field types (this is not a technical requirement for all database tables – it is intended to encourage you to learn about different field types).

2. The following three fields, with the field names exactly as specified, must be included: **CustomerID**, **Last Name**, **Date of Joining**. This ensures that exercises in later topics that are based on the **Customer** table are possible. Your own choice of fields will influence the outcome, but not your ability to achieve a successful outcome.

Some things to think about

Before you approach the keyboard and start inputting a table definition, it is useful to plan out your table definition. This involves the following five stages. The notes below should help you to work through these stages, without telling you exactly what to do.

I. Decide the fields to be included

It is likely that this table will include contact details such as names and addresses. Here is a typical name:

Mrs Jane Susan Akbar

How should this name be entered in the database? The answer to this question depends on the contexts and formats in which you might wish to output the name. Possibilities include: addressing an envelope, entering names into a mail-shot letter, and arranging a list of customers into alphabetical order. If you enter all of this data into one **Name** field you are restricted to using the name in the order and form in which it is entered in the field. Will this be satisfactory for all of the above uses?

Here is a typical address:

Flat 2, 11, Long Acre Meadow, Halwyn, Cornwall, HE3 6RR

How many address fields do you need?

2. Decide on field names

You need to think carefully about field names. It is helpful if field names:

- are easy to remember
- can be used as they stand for labels for printed and on-screen display of data
- are as short as possible.

The exercise below may help you to realise that choosing field names is not as straightforward as it first appears. Below you are given two possible alternative field names for one field. Perhaps with a friend, tick the field name option that you would choose.

Date of Birth		DOB	
Date-Joined		Date joined	
Lastname		Family name	
Sex		Male/Female	
Member No		Customer ID	
Number of bedrooms		No of bedrooms	
Time		Session time	
Occupation		Employment	
City		County	
Membership Number		Member No	
Housetype		Type of House	

3. Decide on field types

Review the discussion of field types in Topic 3. The three fields that you are required to include have the following field types, respectively:

Field Name	Data Type
CustomerID	AutoNumber
Last Name	Text
Date of Joining	Date/Time

Remember that the field type depends upon how you expect to manipulate and see the data in the field. The most common mistakes are associated with numbers. Fields are defined as **Number** fields because you might want to add them up, or perform other mathematical calculations on them. Accordingly, it is unlikely that you will want to define a House Number field or a Telephone Number field as a **Number** field. Such fields are usually most appropriately defined as **Text** fields. Text fields can be displayed, and sorted. Searches can be performed on words in or parts of **Text** fields.

Also remember that long **Memo** fields, whilst at first appearing very flexible, can be difficult to display on screen or in printed reports. A good rule of thumb for getting started is to use only one **Memo** field in each table, and, in general, to think carefully before including **Memo** fields in databases.

4. Decide on field properties

As well as deciding on the field name and a data type for items of data, you can also set field properties. These properties vary slightly according to the data type you have chosen. When you are in table design view you will see the field properties in the lower part of the window. The properties shown will be for the field selected in the top half of the window.

Consider each field you have chosen one at a time:

▨ **Text fields**: field size – how long does the field need to be to accommodate the data in the longest record that you anticipate? Remember that long fields take up space when displayed and can make it more difficult to design screen or print displays. On the other hand, if you are saving an address to print onto an envelope, missing text because the field is too small is unacceptable.

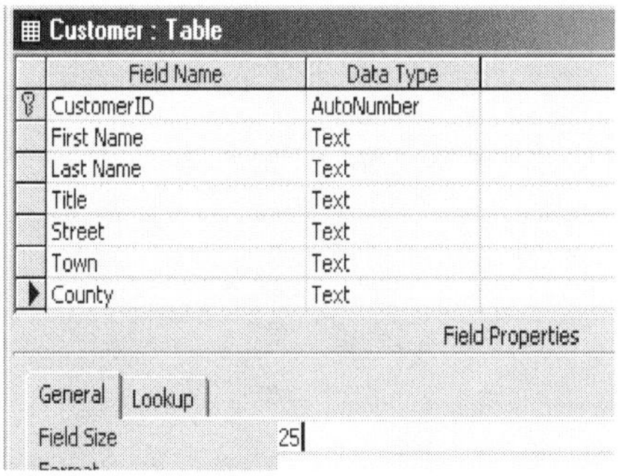

FIGURE 4.1

19

▨ **Number fields**: the default size for number fields is **Long Integer**. If you are planning to use codes to represent categories for a specific field, e.g. 1 for Child, 2 for Teenage, 3 for Adult, and 4 for Senior Citizen, you can make a note about this in the **Description** column. Note that if you wish to record decimal numbers, choose **Field Size** as **Decimal** and then set **Scale** to the number of digits to the *right* of the decimal point that you want displayed.

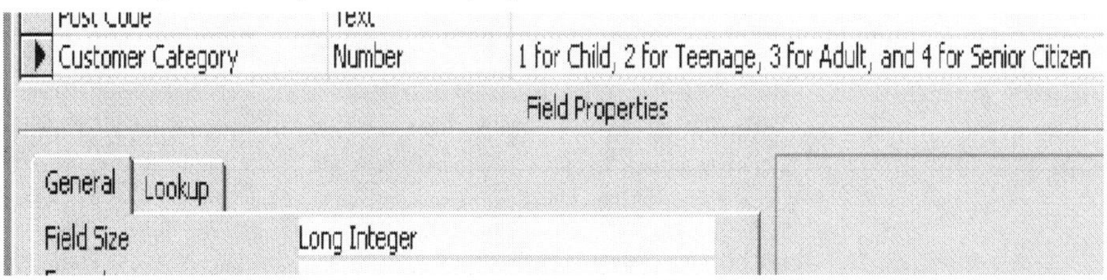

FIGURE 4.2

▨ **Default values**: consider any default values for specific fields. For example, a default value for a County field could be 'Cornwall', since you can be fairly sure that virtually all of the customers of Halwyn Videos will live in Cornwall.

| Default Value | Cornwall |

▨ **Date/Time fields**: decide the format of any such fields. You will probably find **Short Date** most suitable.

FIGURE 4.3

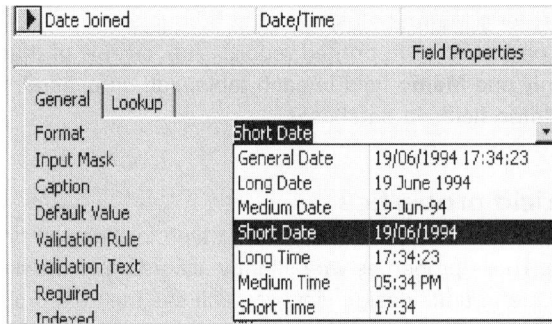

Field types and properties

The table below shows some possible fields for a simple online database of products in a supermarket, such as might be the basis for an online shopping operation. Identify some appropriate field types, field lengths and other properties for each of the fields given.

Table 1. Field types for a product database for an online supermarket

Field name	Example of data
Product ID	123-456
Category	Food
Description	Baked beans
Unit price	25p
Brand	Heinz
Weight	500grams
In-store stock	978
Delivery day	Thursday
Bar code	
Number sold this week	1021

There is no right answer. The objective of this exercise is to demonstrate that you have understood some of the ideas about the definition of table structures. Table structures for the same use (such as a video store) may vary considerably, partly because even businesses in the same industry may use a database differently – unless standards have been agreed for a specific industry sector, as in, for example, airline bookings. In addition, database designers will make their own decisions about how best to design the database. It would be most surprising if your database looked exactly the same as your friend's, or as the database that the authors of this book are using, although there should be some important similarities.

Creating the *Customer* table

Using the design view approach to creating a new table, create the **Customer** table.

1 Starting with the **CustomerID** field, define its type and any field properties.

2 Work through each field in turn. Finally, click on the SAVE button and give this table the name *Customer*. Close the **Table Design Window**.

3 To make a printed copy of the table design, choose **TOOLS-ANALYZE-DOCUMENTER**. If this Wizard is not installed, Access will ask you to install it from the Office CD.

4 Under the **TABLES** tab click on **CUSTOMER**. Click on the **OPTIONS** button and set the following; **Include for Table**: **Properties**; **Include for Fields**: **Names**, **Data types** and **Size**; **Include for Indexes**: **Nothing**. Click on **OK**.

5 Click on **OK** again. If the video table is open you will be prompted to close it. Access will take a few moments to compile the definition, which it will display as a preview. Click on the **PRINT** button to print and close the preview.

We return to the **Customer** table in Topic 5, when we use forms to add data to this table.

Reviewing the *Video* table

1 Open the **Video** table in design view and review the properties of each field.

2 You might wish to alter the field sizes of the **Title**, **Video Category**, and **Censor Rating** fields. Save any changes that you make. Close the table design window. If, later, you find that you need to alter the field sizes, these can be altered in the design view. Take care if you make a field smaller to be sure it is not too small, otherwise you could lose some data.

3 Using the **Documenter** Wizard, print the table definition as for the **Customer** table, this time selecting **VIDEO** under the **TABLES** tab.

21

Portfolio items

Customer table.

Printout of the **Customer** table definition.

Printout of **Video** table definition.

TOPIC 5

Creating and changing data

Topic objectives

Now that you have created and understand table structures, the next step is to explore how those table definitions can be used to contain data. This topic deals with entering data into the database, and making subsequent amendments to the data. Although it is possible to define queries, forms and reports, as discussed in the next few topics, it is not possible to see how these work without some data in the table.

This topic shows you how to:

- use a datasheet to enter data into a table
- navigate around the datasheet so that data can be corrected or changed.

Entering data into the *Video* table

This activity enters data into the table **Video** that you created in Topic 3. To enter data a table needs to be opened in the Datasheet view. You will have encountered Datasheet view in Topic 3, but the preferred approach to table design was through Design view.

To open **Video** in Datasheet view:

1. In the **Database Window**, if **TABLE** is not selected in the **Objects** column, click on it.

2. Double-click the table name, **Video**, or select the table, and click on the **OPEN** button. **Video** will open in Datasheet view. In the Datasheet view the headings of the columns are the field names you previously designed. Each row in the datasheet is a record.

3. You may have some fields already filled in, but at this stage there is little or no data in the table.

4. Do not enter a value into the **VideoID** field but press **ENTER** to move to the next field. **VideoID** is an **AutoNumber** field and if you do try to enter data into it the entry will not be accepted.

5. Enter the data for the **Video** table as shown in Appendix 1 at the end of this book. After entering the data for each field move to the next by pressing **ENTER**, **TAB** or **→**.

6. When you press **ENTER** after entering data into the last field of the first record, Access saves the record.

Leaving a field blank

Sometimes not all the data for a record is available, for example, the telephone number may be missing. To skip a field, simply press **ENTER** or **TAB** to take you to the next field. It is acceptable to skip fields where the data is not vital.

Where a field is left without an entry it is said to be *Null*, i.e. there is nothing there. If you perform mathematical calculations on numeric fields, then Access ignores fields containing nulls.

Using undo

Should you do anything wrong or if something unexpected happens, always try **EDIT-UNDO** or click on the **UNDO** button before doing anything else.

Switching between Datasheet and Design view

Once a table is open it is possible to switch from the Datasheet view to the Design view and vice versa. If you make changes to the design you will be asked to save them before you switch back to the Datasheet view. Use the button at the left of the toolbar for switching between the views.

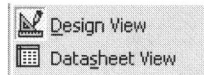

Creating a lookup list

To make data entry less tedious you can create 'lookup' lists which drop down when you click on the field in Datasheet view. In the case of the **Video** table the **Video Category** field is an ideal field for a lookup list. Using a lookup list means that you are consistent in how you enter data and that will mean that queries (Topic 8) will find the relevant records.

1 Open the table **Video** in Design view and select the **Category** field. In the **Field Properties** section in the lower half of the window, click on the **LOOKUP** tab.

2 Open the **Display Control** text box by clicking in it and select **Combo Box**. In the **Row Source Type** box choose **Value List**.

3 In the **Row Source** box type *Action, Drama, Comedy, Drama, Horror, Sci Fi, Children's, Thriller*

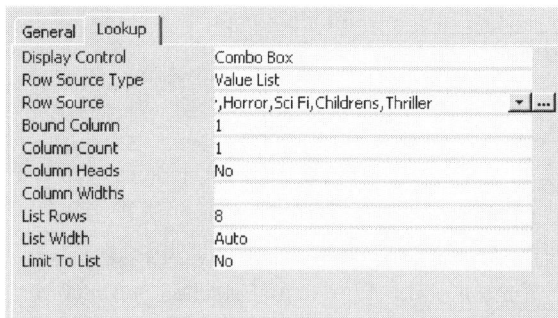

General	Lookup	
Display Control	Combo Box	
Row Source Type	Value List	
Row Source	',Horror,Sci Fi,Childrens,Thriller	
Bound Column	1	
Column Count	1	
Column Heads	No	
Column Widths		
List Rows	8	
List Width	Auto	
Limit To List	No	

FIGURE 5.1

4 Click on the **Datasheet View** button to display the drop-down list you should have just created. Although your table will not have the data illustrated, you should see the drop-down list when you click in a **Video Category** field in the Datasheet view.

FIGURE 5.2

Moving around records in the datasheet

By using either **EDIT-GO TO**, the **UP ARROW** and **DOWN ARROW** keys, **PAGE UP** and **PAGE DOWN** keys, or the vertical scroll bar, you can move between records in the datasheet. However, the most efficient way to move between records in large databases is with the navigation buttons in the lower-left corner of the window.

Access record indicators

In the status bar of the datasheet window are the Access record indicators. Here you will find record movement buttons and the record number of the currently selected record. Clicking the various buttons will move to different records as shown below.

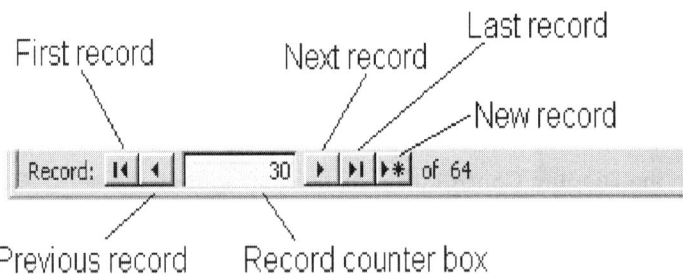

FIGURE 5.3

To go to a specific record, click in the record counter box (or press **F5**), type the record number you want, and then press **ENTER**.

Selecting data

Parts of the datasheet can be selected, so that an operation such as copy or delete can be performed on those parts of the data. Selection of a record makes it possible to delete that record, or to move it elsewhere in the data set. When an area is selected it appears in reverse colour, so if text is normally black on white, then selected text is white on black.

To select	Do this
A single field	Move the pointer to the left hand side of a cell, so that it changes shape into a white cross and click.
A word in a field	Double-click on the word.
A record	Click in the record selector at the left edge of the record, or choose **EDIT-SELECT RECORD**.
More than one record	Click and drag in the record selector edge for the required number of records.
A field column	Click on the column heading (the field name at the top of the column).
Several field columns	Click on the first column heading required for the selection and drag to the last.

Moving and copying fields

A field may be moved, by selecting it, using **EDIT-CUT**, clicking in the cell where the field is to be moved to and using **EDIT-PASTE**.

A field may be copied, by selecting it, using **EDIT-COPY**, clicking in the cell where the copy is required and using **EDIT-PASTE**. You could also use the **CUT**, **COPY** and **PASTE** buttons.

Now try the following exercises:

1 Move around the sheet using the Access record indicators:

- Go to the last record.
- Move up one record to the previous record.
- Repeat.
- Move to the first record.
- Move to the next record.

2 Select the following parts of the data:

- a record
- 3 records together
- a field column
- 3 field columns together
- a single field.

Entering data into the *Customer* table

Enter data for 20 records into your **Customer** table, working through records in whatever is the most convenient order. Remember that:

- For the fields **Last Name,** and **Date of Joining,** the data should be entered as in the first 20 records in the **Customer** table shown in Appendix 1.

For the remainder of the fields in your table, make up the data to be entered.

Portfolio items

Video table – with lookup list for **Video Category** and data entered.

Customer table – with data entered.

Amending data

Topic objectives

Data in a database is not usually static. New data in the form of new records will be added periodically; data in existing records will need to be kept up to date; and records that are no longer required will need to be removed. This topic will show you how to:

- check data for errors
- amend existing records
- delete records.

Checking data for errors

What happens if a mistake is made when data is being input? For example, what if £109.9 is entered for the cost of a video instead of £10.99? Some checking or *validation* is carried out already to prevent you from, say, entering text into a date or numeric field. To check for valid data, Access allows you to create rules. For example, the rule <50 (less than 50) would prevent a cost of £50 or more being entered into the **Cost** field.

To set up this *validation rule*:

1 Display the **Video** table in Design view. Select the **Cost** field and in the field properties, key in <50 in the **Validation Rule** box.

2 If the validation rule is broken, i.e. someone types in a cost of over £50, then Access can display a message. You set the text of that message by filling in the **Validation Text** box as illustrated below.

3 Save the table, click **YES** to checking existing data, open the datasheet and deliberately enter a cost of over £50. You should see your message. Click **OK** and press **ESC** to restore the original value.

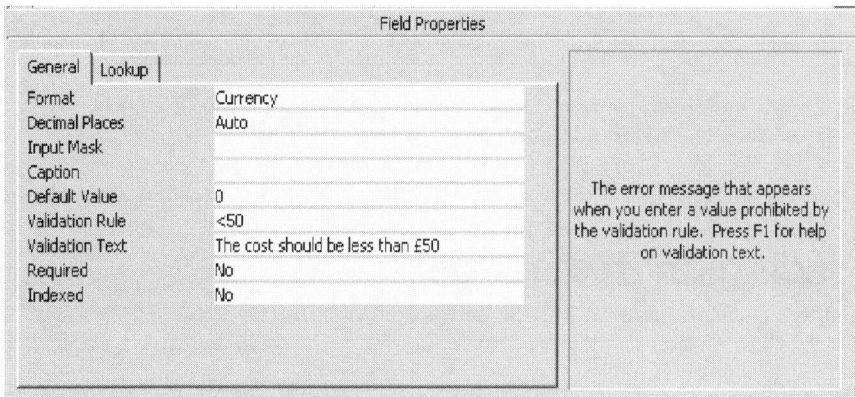

Field Properties	
General Lookup	
Format	Currency
Decimal Places	Auto
Input Mask	
Caption	
Default Value	0
Validation Rule	<50
Validation Text	The cost should be less than £50
Required	No
Indexed	No

The error message that appears when you enter a value prohibited by the validation rule. Press F1 for help on validation text.

FIGURE 6.1

Using the spell checker

With the data displayed in the datasheet, you may spell check by clicking on the **SPELLING** button [ABC]. The spell checker will prompt you to correct words that it does not recognise. Click on the **IGNORE** button if you do not want it to change the word.

FIGURE 6.2

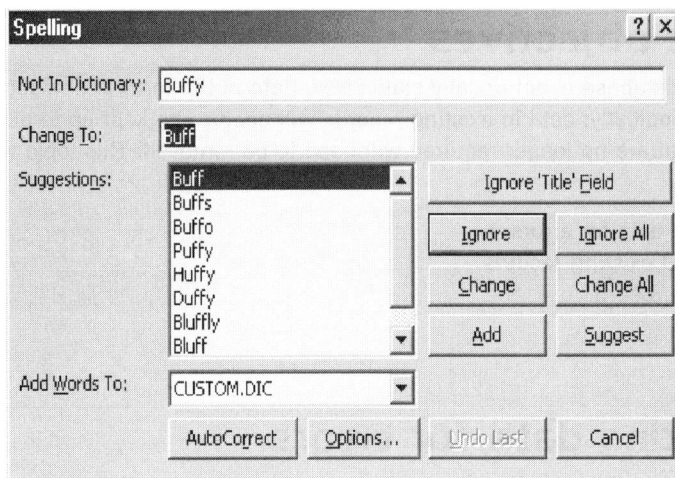

To correct a mistake, select the correction from the **Suggestions** box, and click on the **CHANGE** button.

28

FIGURE 6.3

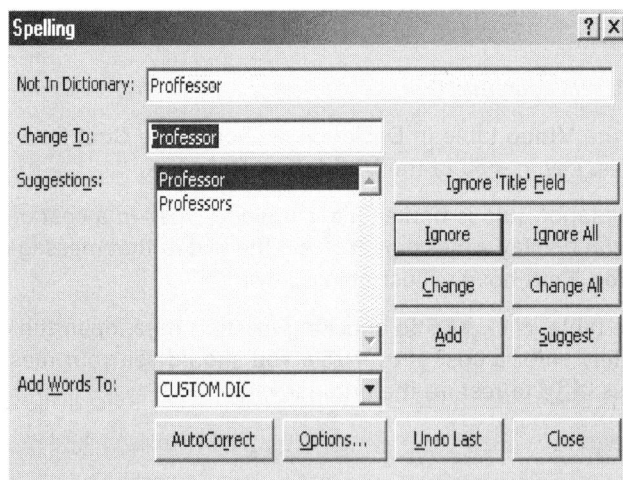

1 Open the **Video** table in Datasheet view and check the spellings.

Finding an item of data

To find a particular item in a field use the command **EDIT-FIND**.

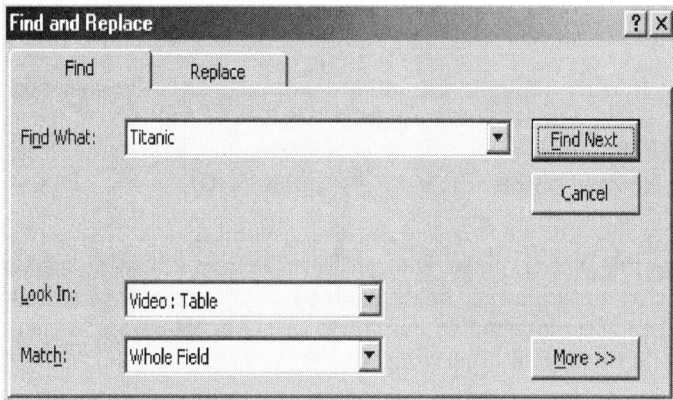

FIGURE 6.4

Key the string (set of characters) you wish to find into the **FIND WHAT** text box, such as the video title 'Titanic'. In the **Match:** box, select whether your string should match the whole field, any part of the field or the start of the field.

Click on the **FIND NEXT** button. If you want to continue the search for this item, click on **FIND NEXT** again. Each time a match is found it is highlighted. If either the top or the bottom of the table is reached, Access indicates that there are no more matches to be found.

29

Replacing data

To replace a particular field, click on the **REPLACE** tab of the **Find and Replace** dialog box or use **EDIT-REPLACE**. The steps are the same as for finding a field, except that in the dialog box there is an additional text box, **Replace With**, into which the replacement text is entered. Replacements are made according to which button is clicked:

| Replace | Replaces the highlighted text and finds the next occurrence of the contents of the **Find What** box. |
| Replace All | Replaces all occurrences of the string without stopping. Use this with care as unexpected replacements can happen. |

Amending existing records

If some of the details of a record change, such as a customer's address, has changed then the datasheet can be edited.

1 Open your **Customer** table in Datasheet view. Pick the last name of one of the records. Use **EDIT–FIND** in the name column and enter the customer's name. If you want Access to match with part of the field then select the appropriate option in the **Match** text box. Click **FIND NEXT** until Access picks out the

required record. You might think this is 'overkill', but what if there were hundreds of records in the table?

2 Tab across to the address field and make some amendments assuming that one (or more) customers has a change of address. You do not have to do a save operation as Access automatically saves changes to records. Note that you cannot alter the **AutoNumber** field (**CustomerID**).

3 You might like to try a find and replace operation with this datasheet. You could, for instance, replace 'Halwyn Bay' (**Town** field) with 'Helston'. If the town is part of an address field, use the **match any part of the field** option in the **Find and Replace** dialog box. This is an unrealistic replacement, but recent changes to telephone numbers could easily be carried out using this method.

Deleting records

You will need to delete records as they become obsolete, for example, a video that is damaged will need to be removed from the list. A customer who withdraws their membership could also be deleted.

You can delete a record from a table using a datasheet or a form. (You will meet forms in Topic 11.)

To delete records using a datasheet, first display the datasheet.

FIGURE 6.5

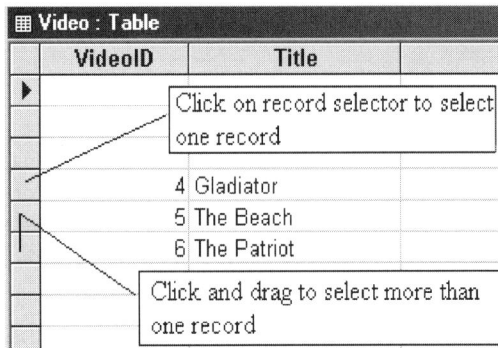

Select the record or records you wish to delete. Select one record by clicking its record selector or select several records by clicking a record selector and dragging down the required number of rows. Press the **DELETE** key (or choose **EDIT-DELETE**).

Access prompts you to confirm the deletion. Choose **YES** to delete the record or **NO** to cancel the delete operation. Once you say yes there is no going back, you will have to re-enter the data into a new record or records.

FIGURE 6.6

If you delete a record that uses an **AutoNumber** field, such as one of the records in the **Video** table, Access will not use that number in **VideoID** again. Access will allocate the next unused number to the **VideoID** field of any new records thus ensuring that every record has a different **VideoID** number.

Try the following exercises:

1 Add a few more customer records to the customer table and then delete, first a single record and then two records together. If you have used an **AutoNumber** field for the **CustomerID** field, note the effect.

2 This exercise is designed to reinforce your ability to create a table and to use cut and paste with records.

- Add some more records to the **Customer** table. Create a new table exactly like the **Customer** table and call it *Archived Customer*.
- Open the **Customer** table in Datasheet view, select a record and use **EDIT-CUT**. Open the **Archived Customer** table in Datasheet view and use **EDIT-PASTE**. You should have pasted in the record you have removed from the **Customer** table.
- Close both tables. Archiving data is useful to remove non-current data from a table without permanently deleting it. Archived data can provide historical information such as a sales history. It can also be useful to restore a record removed by mistake. Generally, for small databases you would not need to archive data, but you may wish to consider why large organisations such as banks would want to be careful about archiving data.

31

Portfolio item

Archived Customer table.

Changing and reorganising data

Topic objectives

The datasheet is your 'view' on the data held in the table. It can be used to enter, print and amend data.

This topic show you how to:

- control the look of the datasheet
- sort and filter data in the datasheet
- print data from the datasheet.

Altering column widths

By altering the width of columns and the height of rows in the datasheet, the display of data can be tailored to show the data in a suitable fashion.

1 Open the **Video** table in Datasheet view. To alter the **Title** column width, move the pointer to the field name row at the top of the datasheet, between **Title** and **Year of Release**. The pointer should change shape to a ✛.

2 Click and drag the column to widen it. Try adjusting other column widths of the **Video** datasheet to accommodate the data. Where appropriate, you could make columns narrower rather than wider.

3 If you close the datasheet, Access will ask you if you wish to save the changes you have made. It does not matter whether you choose to save the changes or not for any of the changes suggested in this topic.

Data display – fonts

1 With the **Video** table datasheet open, choose **FORMAT-FONT** and select a font, size and colour from the **Font** dialog box.

FIGURE 7.1 **2** All the data will take on the selected font. It is not possible to apply fonts independently to fields or columns. You may wish to use **UNDO** to return to the original font.

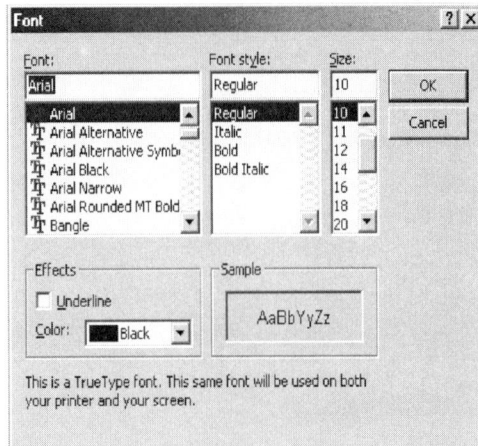

3 Access will ask you if you wish to save these changes when you close the datasheet.

Datasheet formatting

The look of the datasheet can be altered using the **FORMAT-DATASHEET** command.

1 Open the **Video** table in Datasheet view. Choose **FORMAT-DATASHEET** and the **Datasheet Formatting** dialog box is displayed.

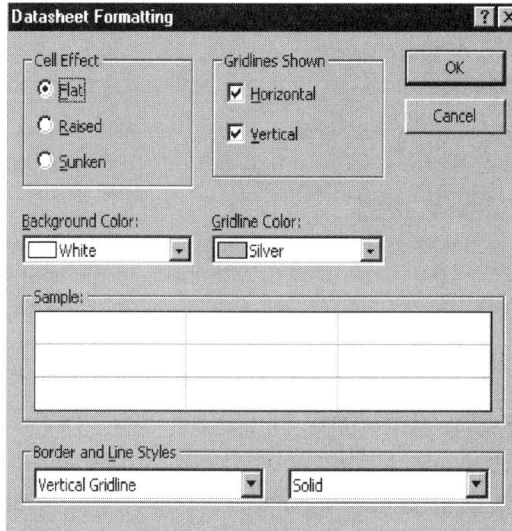

FIGURE 7.2

2 Select the **Raised** cell effect and click on **OK**. Use the formatting command again and look at the **Sunken** effect. There are more options available if you choose the **Flat** effect, such as colour and style of the dividing lines.

33

3 Select some formatting of your choice. When you close the datasheet you will be prompted to save the formatting changes and you can either save them or discard them. Avoid colours that do not contrast well, especially if you are printing.

Data display – sorting

The data in a datasheet will be displayed in 'natural order', that is in the order in which the records were entered. It does not matter in what order the records are entered because they can be displayed in any order you require using the **SORT ASCENDING** and **SORT DESCENDING** buttons on the toolbar.

To change the displayed order of the records using one field:

1 Open the **Video** table in Datasheet view. Select the **Title** column as the one by which you wish to sort by clicking on the field name at the top of the column.

2 Click on either the **SORT ASCENDING** or **SORT DESCENDING** button. Try this for other fields in the table, such as **Category** and **Censor Rating**.

Changing the order of columns in the datasheet

To rearrange the order in which the columns are shown in the datasheet, use a drag and drop method to move them.

1 First select the field column you wish to move, move the pointer over the selection so that it changes shape to a left-pointing arrow, click (pointer changes shape to drag and drop) and drag the column to a new position. A darker column dividing line will indicate where the field will go when the mouse button is released.

2 Select the **Censor Rating** column and drag it to be positioned to the right of the **Category** column.

To change the displayed sort order of the records using more than one field, select the columns by which you wish to sort (click on the field name at the top of the first column and drag to the last column). Sorting columns must be next to one another with the highest priority being assigned to the left-most column. To achieve the required sorting it may be necessary to rearrange the columns as described above.

3 Select the **Category** and **Censor Rating** columns together and click on the **SORT ASCENDING** button. Note the effect.

4 Close the **Video** table datasheet. Save changes if you wish.

Selecting records using a filter

As well as sorting records in the datasheet, Access allows you to select records in the datasheet using a filtering process. The simplest way to use a filter is to click on field data that you want to select and click on the **FILTER BY SELECTION** button in the toolbar. Only those records that contain the same item of data in that field will be selected and displayed. The other records are still there, but they are hidden from view.

Filter by Selection

Remove/Apply Filter

1 Open the **Video** table in Datasheet view, click in any data item 'Comedy' in the **Category** column, and click on the **FILTER BY SELECTION** button to apply a filter to display only records in the Comedy category.

2 To remove the filter, click on the **REMOVE FILTER** button. Note that once the filter is removed this button becomes an **APPLY FILTER** button and can be used to re-apply the filter.

3 You can further refine the filter by making subsequent selections. For example, display all the comedy category records as before and then choose a **Censor Rating** and click on the **FILTER BY SELECTION** button again.

4 Filters can be saved with tables so you will be prompted by Access to save the table when you close it, but as we do not want to save the filter say **NO** to this.

Excluding data

You can filter by excluding a selection.

1 Open the **Video** table in datasheet view, right-click in any data item '18' in the **Censor Rating** column and choose **FILTER EXCLUDING SELECTION** from the shortcut menu to apply a filter to display all records that are not an 18 certificate.

| Filter By Selection |
| Filter Excluding Selection |
| Filter For: |
| Remove Filter/Sort |

Printing a datasheet

A table can be printed from its datasheet. Access prints a datasheet as it appears on the screen. It is advisable always to preview your datasheet before printing by choosing **FILE-PRINT PREVIEW** or clicking on the **PRINT PREVIEW** button in the toolbar.

Printing all the records

1 To print all the records in the **Video** table, open the **Video** table in Datasheet view.

2 Choose **FILE-PRINT PREVIEW**, to preview all records. You can 'zoom-in' and 'zoom-out' on the preview page by clicking on it.

3 You may find that the records would fit better if printed in landscape orientation. To change orientation use **FILE-PAGE SETUP** and select the **LANDSCAPE** option. If the columns are the wrong width, close the preview window and adjust the column widths before previewing again.

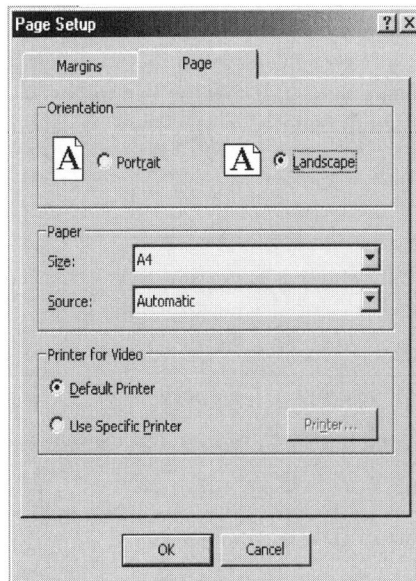

FIGURE 7.3

4 When the preview is satisfactory and if you wish to print, choose **FILE-PRINT** to display the **Print** dialog box and click on **OK**.

Printing records in a sorted order

Sort the records so that they are in category order using the **ASCENDING** button. Select a different font and (if you have a colour printer) colour. Adjust column widths if necessary. Repeat the printing process above to print out the sorted records.

Printing filtered records

When records in the datasheet are filtered, only the selected records will be printed. Apply a filter that selects a particular category and a particular censor rating. Choose a suitable font, column widths and orientation before printing.

Sorting, selecting and printing the *Customer* table

For the following printouts select suitable fonts, column widths and orientation:

- Print all the records in the **Customer** table in last name alphabetical order.
- Print all the records in the **Customer** table in date of joining order. If you did not use a 'Date' type for this field or your table does not have this field see Topic 11 about modifying tables.
- Use a filter to select some records, for example, customers in a particular town or with the same last name. You may wish to add to or modify your records so that this filter will select two or three records. Print the result of your selection.

Note: For large datasheets, Microsoft Access prints from left to right and then from top to bottom. For example, if your datasheet is two pages wide and three pages long, Microsoft Access prints the top two pages first, then the middle two pages, then the bottom two pages.

Portfolio items

Printout of all **Video** table records.

Printout of all **Video** records sorted in **Category** order.

Printout of **Video** records filtered by **Category** and **Censor Rating**.

Printout of **Customer** table in Last Name order.

Printout of **Customer** table in Date of Joining order.

Printout of filtered **Customer** table.

Basic queries

Topic objectives

Queries allow you to retrieve sets of records from a table or database according to a set of criteria. You may, for example, want to identify all of the videos in a specific category. A query can be formulated to select such records. If a query is saved it can be used at a later date, or on a regular basis, to select from an updated database, or to identify new records that have been added to the database in a specific category.

This topic will show you how to:

- use the Query Wizard to create simple queries
- view the results of using a query
- be able to save a query so that it can be used again
- print the output from a query.
- delete a query.

What are queries?

Queries have a very important role in database systems, because they are the main means by which data can be extracted or retrieved. Remember that, although you can scan the small test table that you are creating in this book, most real databases have numerous tables, each with thousands, millions or billions of records. Finding the record or information that you want in such a database is akin to looking for a needle in a haystack. Queries are essential for retrieval in such databases. They are used in:

- Searching for and retrieving specific records. For example, to look at a particular set of members' records for editing, or to view the videos on loan to a specific individual.
- Creating forms and printing reports. Queries retrieve a particular set of records and fields; reports are used to print this information. A form based on a query can be used to restrict data entry to certain fields.
- Drawing together data from several tables within the database. For example, to create an invoice an address may be extracted from one table, and the order details from another. The examples that we work with here are based only on the **Video** table.

In order to create a query it is necessary to select both the fields and the records to be included in the query:

- **Selecting the records** – Query or search criteria must be used to select the records to be included in the query output. These criteria have to be based on the data in the records. Access provides a method of querying by which you can describe the characteristics of the data that you are looking for. This method is know as Query By Example (QBE) and is achieved by allowing you to give examples of the data that you are searching for, which form the search criteria.
- **Selecting the fields** – It is not usually necessary to retrieve all fields. For example,

only the number and title of a video may be sufficient for a list of videos that is intended to be used as a check-list in stocktaking. Access offers a means of indicating which fields are to be shown in any query output listing.

Using the Simple Query Wizard

The Simple Query Wizard helps you design a simple select query. A select query will select fields from a table. It does not allow you to apply search criteria, and is therefore very limited in its usefulness, but it is useful to introduce the Simple Query Wizard here, so that we can create a query, and practise with the Query Design window, running and viewing a query, and saving, printing and deleting a query.

The Wizard will ask you to select the table you wish to query and which fields you want in your query. It will create the query, which you can then modify later using the **Query Design Window**.

To create a query on the **Video** table:

1 From the **Database Window** choose QUERIES from the **Objects** column and click on the NEW button. Choose the Simple Query Wizard from the NEW QUERY dialog box. Click on OK. **Note**: If you have not created any queries yet then the OPEN and DESIGN buttons are not available.

2 From the TABLE/QUERIES drop-down list in the SIMPLE QUERY WIZARD dialog box select the **Video** table.

3 This will display the dialog box below. To add the selected fields to the query, highlight each field and click on the > button. You may change your mind and use the << button to remove all fields (so you may start again) or use the < button to remove a selected field. Add the fields **VideoID, Title, Video Category**, and **Censor Rating** to the query by highlighting each field in turn and clicking on the > button.

4 Click on NEXT>. Select a **Detail** query and click on NEXT>. Give the query the file name *Stock Check List* and click on FINISH. The result of your query will be shown in Datasheet view. View and close the query window, and the name of the query is listed as a **Queries Object** in the **Database Window**.

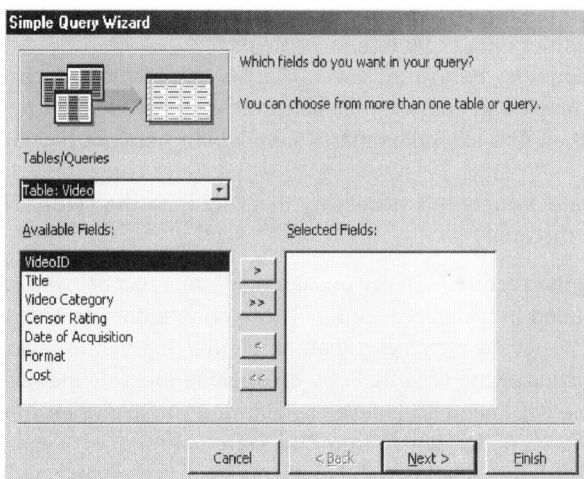

FIGURE 8.1

Adding fields to a query using the Query Design Window

The Query Design Window is more flexible than the Simple Query Wizard because it allows you to design both the field and the records to be included in the query. This window is in two sections:

- The upper section is where the table windows of the tables used in the query are displayed.
- The lower section is a grid for the query design. The two most important rows in the grid are **Field** and **Criteria**. Each column needs a field name and all the fields in the table may be chosen or a only few of them. In the **Criteria** row an example of the data may be given.

As you will see, the business of specifying a query is more complex than entering a phrase of two or three words into a search engine, and sending the search engine out across the Web to locate websites to satisfy your query. Although this is a context in which a large database is being searched, the structure and contents of the websites are not standardised, and so the search engine needs to use complex algorithms to produce the best match that it can between the query and the search output. You will know that this often leads to all sorts of websites being retrieved that are not very useful in the context of the query. This type of retrieval is rather an imprecise art, because of the diversity of the data being searched.

The kind of imprecision that is characteristic of Web searching is not acceptable in searching business databases. For example, it would be unacceptable to mail a promotion for an adult video to a child member, or to leave some of the members who had not used the store for a while out of a mailing to encourage such members to renew their use of the store. This means that specifying queries in this context must be precise, and can sometimes be complex.

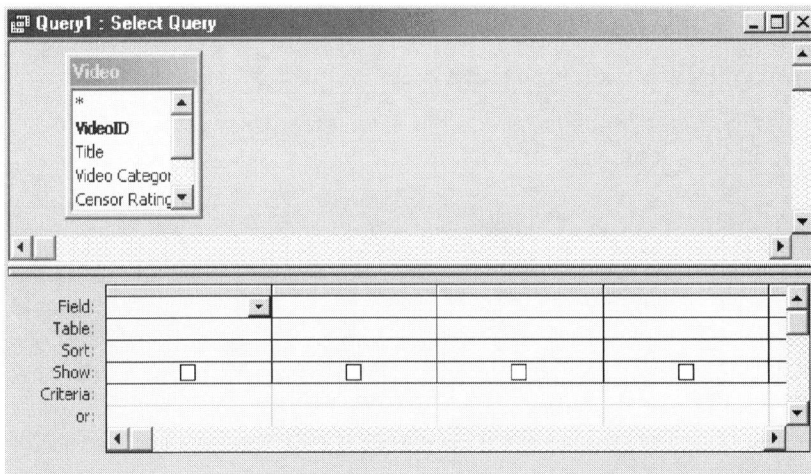

FIGURE 8.2

First we will practise using the Query Design Window. To open the Query Design Window:

1. From the Database window choose **QUERIES** from the **Objects** column and click on the **NEW** button to create a new query.

2. Select **DESIGN VIEW** in the **NEW QUERY** dialog box and click on **OK**.

3 The **Show Table** dialog box appears in front of the query design window. This dialog box allows you to select all the tables needed for the query. Select the **Video** table and choose ADD to add it to the query.

Now experiment with the methods of adding fields from the **Video** table to the query described below. You want to finish with a query called **Stock Currency**, which has the following fields: **Title, Date of Acquisition, Cost, Format.**

The simplest case of adding fields to a query is when we want to include all the fields in the table.

1 Double-click on the title bar of the field list box of the table in the upper section of the window. This selects all the fields.

2 Click on any of the selected fields (not the *) and drag to the field cell in the lower section of the Query window. The pointer should look like a set of record cards.

3 When you release the mouse button, all the field names will have been added to the query. Use the horizontal scroll bar to move to the right, as all the columns will not fit on the screen.

Sometimes we do not wish to add all fields to a query.

There are three ways of adding the fields one by one to a query:

The first method is by double-clicking, thus:

1 Double-click on the name of the field required in the field list box in the upper section of the window. It will appear in the next available column in the grid below.

The second method is to use the drop-down list associated with each field cell, thus:

1 Click in the field cell in the lower section of the window. A list box button appears at the end of the cell.

2 Click on the list box button and a drop-down list of field names will appear.

3 Select the name of the field required. If necessary, scroll through the list, click on it and it will appear in the field cell.

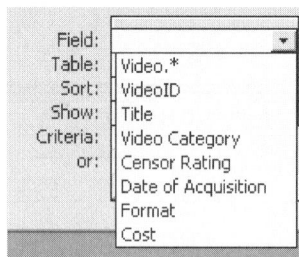

FIGURE 8.3

Field:	
Table:	Video.*
Sort:	VideoID
Show:	Title
Criteria:	Video Category
or:	Censor Rating
	Date of Acquisition
	Format
	Cost

The third way is to use the drag-and-drop method, thus:

1 Click on the name of the field required in the field list box in the upper section of the window.

2 Drag and drop this field into the required field cell in the lower part of the Query window. While doing this, the pointer should look like one record card.

3 If you drop the field onto a column containing a field, then a column will be inserted to contain the new field.

Fields may be removed singly or in blocks from the query.

To remove the all the fields from the query:

1 Select the first column by clicking on the bar at the top of the column (the pointer will change shape to a down arrow) and drag to select all the columns.

2 Press the **DELETE** key or choose **EDIT-DELETE**.

To remove an individual field from the query, just select the required column for deleting and use **EDIT-DELETE**.

Viewing or running a query

1 To see the result of your query, **Stock currency**, either click on the **VIEW DATA** button or the **RUN QUERY** button in the toolbar.

2 To return to the query design, click on the **VIEW DESIGN** button.

View design button ▨ ▾ View data button ▦ ▾ Run Query button !

Access displays a datasheet containing the records that match the query with fields as defined in the query. Access calls this query result a *dynaset*. A dynaset is a temporary table and is not a permanent part of your database. If you modify your query, the resulting dynaset will change accordingly.

41

Saving a query

Sometimes you may wish to ask the same question of a database over and over again. For example, suppose that you wish to send regular monthly announcements of all new U films to customers who are children. Both the **Customer** and the **Video** tables will change from month to month as new videos are acquired, and members come and go. This activity will requires two queries:

▨ a query to identify those members who are children, to be performed on the **Customer** table

▨ a query to identify new U-rated videos performed on the **Video** table.

Both of these queries will need to be executed on a monthly basis. To save any of the queries that you currently have open:

1 Choose **FILE-SAVE**.

2 In the **QUERY NAME** box of the **SAVE AS** dialog box, enter a name that will remind you what the query is about. The name can be up to 255 characters. Click on **OK**.

3 If you close the Query window, you will see the name of your query in the Queries list of the Database window, from where it can be opened for use on another occasion.

Closing and opening a query

To close a query, either double-click on the query's control menu button, or choose **FILE-CLOSE**.

You can open an existing query in either Design view or Datasheet view.

To open a query in **Design** view:

1 In the Database window, click on the **QUERY** button.

2 Select the Query you want to open, and then click on the **DESIGN** button.

To open a query in **Datasheet** view:

1 In the Database window, click on the **QUERY** button.

2 Select the Query you want to open, and then click on the **OPEN** button.

Printing a query

It is often useful to print the output from a query. Here we will print the dynaset produced by the query **Stock Check List.**

1 From the Database window open the query in Datasheet view.

2 In the Datasheet view, click on the **PRINT PREVIEW** button on the toolbar. You will be shown a preview, which displays a miniature version of what is to be printed.

3 The pointer becomes a magnifying glass and can be use to zoom-in to the page. If you use other Windows applications you will be familiar with this. Clicking will 'toggle' between zoom-in and zoom-out modes. When zoomed-in, the vertical and horizontal scroll bars can be used to scroll around your previewed page.

4 Some columns may need widening. To adjust the column widths you need to return to the Datasheet view. To do this click on the **CLOSE** button. The column widths are adjusted in the same way as for table datasheets.

5 Click on **CLOSE** to return to the datasheet and widen the columns.

6 Preview again and zoom in to check that the columns are wide enough.

7 Choose **FILE-PRINT**. The **PRINT** dialog box appears. If you want to print without changing anything then skip the following three steps.

Note: To print directly without displaying the **PRINT** dialog box then click on the **PRINT** button in the toolbar.

8 In the **PRINT** dialog box click on the **SETUP** button and the **PAGE SETUP** dialog box appears.

9 To change the margins, click in the appropriate box and edit the default setting. You can select the orientation of the page, the printer and the paper size. The **PRINT HEADINGS** check box, if not checked, will suppress the printing of the field names as headings. Click on **OK** to return to the **PRINT** dialog box.

10 Click on **OK** in the **PRINT** dialog box and the dynaset should be printed. An extract of the top of the page is shown below.

11 Click on the **CLOSE** button to return to the Datasheet view.

Stock Check List   01/06/2001

VideoID	Title	Video Category	Censor Rating
2	Deep Blue Sea	Drama	18
3	Buffy Series III	Sci Fi	15
4	Gladiator	Action	15
5	The Beach	Drama	15
6	The Patriot	Action	15
7	Big Momma's House	Comedy	12
8	Perfect Storm	Drama	12
9	Mission: Impossible 2	Action	15

FIGURE 8.4

Deleting a query

Some queries may only be used once, in which case it is not really worth saving them. Queries that will be used more than once should be saved, but a query may outlive its usefulness or be superseded by another query. Such queries should be deleted.

Note: Care needs to be taken when removing a query. If reports or forms are based on a query that is deleted, these also become redundant, and should also be deleted.

To delete a query, in the Database window click on the **QUERIES** tab to display the queries. Highlight the query that is to be deleted and press the **DELETE** key.

43

More practice in creating simple queries

1 Create a series of queries showing all of the records in the **Customer** table, but including only the following fields:

- **CustomerID, Title, First Name, Last Name, Telephone No.** Save this query as *CustomersTelephone*.
- **CustomerID, Date of Joining.** Save this query as *CustomersJoin*.
- **Title, Last Name, Street, Town, County, Post Code.** Save this query as *CustomersAddress*.

2 Examine each of the dynasets in turn. Discuss circumstances in which each of these lists may be useful.

Portfolio items

Stock Check List (electronic and printout).

Stock Currency query.

CustomersTelephone query.

CustomersJoin query.

CustomersAddress query.

More simple queries

Topic objectives

In the previous topic you created some simple queries using the Query Wizard, and explored how to specify the fields to be included in the output from a query. In this topic, you will experiment with using queries to select specific sets of records. To do this you will use some simple query criteria. Such queries are important for defining the data to be displayed in reports and forms.

This topic will show you how to:

- create simple queries using query criteria
- explore a range of query criteria on different fields, and with different field types
- sort the output from queries
- perform simple formatting on the output from queries.

Entering query criteria

Query criteria basically allow the enquirer to frame questions, which enable specific records to be retrieved from the database. We might want to find out various things using the data stored in a table. For example, some questions that might be asked about the **Video** table are:

- Which videos are in the Horror category?
- Which videos are in DVD format?
- Which videos have a censor rating of 18?
- Which videos were acquired over two years ago?
- It is possible to locate the video with the title 'Jurassic Park'?

Query criteria need to be entered in the data format for the field that is being searched. This activity shows you how to perform queries using the data types **Text**, **Date** and **Yes/No**.

1 Create a new query using the **Video** table.

2 Add all the fields to the query.

Which videos are in the Horror category?

1 In the Criteria cell of the **Video Category** field, type *Horror*.

2 Click on the **DATASHEET** or **RUN** button. The resulting dynaset should only contain records for which the **Video Category** field is equal to Horror.

Video Category
Video
☑
Horror

3 Save the query as *Horror*. Print the query output.

Note: Before creating the next query you need to ensure that you have removed the previous query criteria. To do this, if necessary, return to Design view, and delete the criterion **Horror**. Select the cell by double-clicking and press **DELETE** to clear the cell. Alternatively, click in the cell and use the `BACKSPACE` key to delete the criterion.

Which videos are in DVD format?

1 In the **Criteria** cell of the **Format** field, type **No**. This field is a **Yes/No** datatype and ticks indicate Yes. We are using Yes to mean VHS so to pick out the DVDs we need to type in **No**. You may need to scroll to the right to display this cell on the screen.

Format
Video
☑
No

2 Click on the **DATASHEET** or **RUN** button and view the resulting dynaset.

3 Save this query as **DVD**. Print the query.

Which videos have a censor rating of 18?

1 For this query we will also identify specific fields to be included in the output, and perform simple formatting on the output. Don't forget to delete any earlier criteria. Then, in the **Criteria** cell of the **Censor Rating** field, type *18*.

2 Adjust the fields included in the query (see Topic 8) so that only the **Title**, the **Censor Rating** and the **Date of Acquisition** are included.

Title	Censor Rating	Date of Acquisition
Video	Video	Video
☑	☑	☑
	"18"	

3 Click on the **DATASHEET** or **RUN** button and view the resulting dynaset. Experiment with changing the font on the dynaset form in the same way as you formatted the datasheet fonts in Topic 7.

4 Print the query. Save the query as **Censor18**.

Which videos were acquired over two years ago?

1 First you need to translate this query into a form that you can use with the data in the table. Let's say that this means that we are interested in all videos that have a Date of Acquisition before 1/1/2000. In the **Criteria** cell of the **Date of Acquisition** field, type **<1/1/2000**.

VideoID	Title	Date of Acquisition
Video	Video	Video
☑	☑	☑
		<1/1/2000

2 Include only the fields **Date of Acquisition**, **VideoID**, and **Title**.

3 Click on the **DATASHEET** or **RUN** button and view the resulting dynaset.

4 Sort the records in the dynaset by the **Date of Acquisition**, by, in the dynaset view, selecting the **Date of Acquisition** column by clicking on the field name at the top of the column. Click on the **SORT DESCENDING** button (for additional guidance see Topic 7).

⑤ Perform any formatting on the query that will make the printout match your house style. Print the query. Save the query as *OldVids*.

Is it possible to locate the record for the video with the title `Jurrasic Park'?

This query is an additional query on a text field in order to demonstrate how you might find an individual record on the basis of a title. (Filters could also be used for this application.)

① In the **Criteria** cell of the **Title** field type *Jurassic Park*.

② Click on the **DATASHEET** or **RUN** button and view the resulting dynaset.

③ Print the query dynaset. Save the query as *Jurassic*.

Title
Video
☑
Jurassic Park

Mathematical operators in query criteria

The following table summarises the basic mathematical operators that can be used in queries.

Operator	Meaning
Mathematical operators	
<	less than
>	greater than
< >	not equal to
> =	greater than or equal to
< =	less than or equal to

① Create a new query using the **Video** table. Add the fields **Title**, **Category**, **Censor Rating** and **Cost** to the query.

② Using the **Cost** field, try the following criteria **<6** to find cost up to £5.99, **<=6** to find cost up to £6.00.

③ Using the **Censor Rating** field, try the following criterion: **<>PG** to find all videos not in this category.

Renaming and hiding fields in a query

When queries are printed it is sometimes necessary to widen the column so that the field name at the top of the column can be seen. This can lead to unnecessarily wide columns, so it is useful to be able to rename the field. The field header can be renamed in a query with an alternative name. For example, **Acquisition Date** instead of **Date of Acquisition**.

To change field header names:

- Switch to Query Design mode by clicking on the **QUERY DESIGN** button. Move the insertion point to the column containing the field header name you wish to change.
- Point to the beginning of the field header and click. The aim is to put the flashing insertion point at the beginning of the header name.
- If you accidentally select the header, press ⌨F2⌨ to de-select it. If the insertion point is not at the beginning, then press the ⌨HOME⌨ key to move it to the first character position.

Acquisition Date: Date of Acquisition
Video
☑

- Type in the new name for the field, and follow the name with a colon (:). Do not put a space between the name and the colon. The colon separates the name you type from the existing field name, which moves to the right to make room for your addition.
- Click on the **DATASHEET** button or the **RUN QUERY** button and the query result with amended field header will be displayed.

Note: Remember that renaming the field in the query header does not affect the name of the field in the underlying table.

To be able to impose a criterion on a field, that field needs to be in the query grid, which means that it will form part of the dynaset. This may not always be desirable, so Access offers the choice of whether or not the field forms part of the dynaset. By default, all fields in the query show in the dynaset as the **Show** cell is on. Sometimes it may not be desirable to display the field on which the query has been performed in the output. You can hide a field by clicking in the box in the **Show** cell. The tick disappears and the field will not form part of the dynaset.

The exercise below also shows how you can apply criteria to more than one field in a query.

The following query lists **the names and addresses of all the adult members who joined since 1/3/2001.**

Note: If your **Customer** table does not allow you to perform this query exactly as specified, make up your own query that uses two query criteria. Perform the renaming and hiding activities on this query.

1. Create a new query using the **Customer** table.

2. Add the following fields: **CustomerID, Title, Lastname, Street, Town, County, Post Code, Member Type, Date of Joining**.

3. In the criteria field of **Member Type**, create a criteria that selects all Adult members.

4. In the criteria field of **Date of Joining**, create a criteria that selects all members who joined since 1/3/2001.

5. Hide both of these fields by clicking in their respective **Show** cells.

6. Sort the **Lastname** field in ascending order.

7. Rename **Lastname** as **Family name** (as indicated above). Display the dynaset.

	CustomerID	Title	Family Name	Street	Town	County	Post Code
▶	36 Mr		Tayshun	46 Greenbank Drive	Halwyn Bay	Cornwall	HE5 6HL
	37	Miss	Breaks	19 Park Road	Halwyn Bay	Cornwall	HE6 5GF
	39	Mr	Dewer	46 Beechwood Road	Halwyn Bay	Cornwall	HE6 4GH
*	(AutoNumber)					Cornwall	

8. Save the query as *New Members*. Close the query.

More queries

Here are a few more queries that you could try for practice. They are based on the **Customer** table. If your tutor asks you to submit the output from these queries as part of your portfolio, then you will need to save each query. Otherwise, just perform the query, undertake any necessary formatting, print the query output if you like, and close the query. These queries are on the **Customer** table so you may need to adjust the queries to match the data in your table.

1. Produce a list of the names and addresses of all of the customers who live in **Helston**.

2. Produce a list of all of the customers **who joined in the last six months**. Sort this list into date order. Include the fields: **CustomerID, Title, Last Name** and **Telephone No**, but not the **Date Joined** field.

3. Produce a list of **all the male customers, which shows their names and addresses**. Sort the list into order by **Last Name**.

4. Produce **three separate lists of the customers in each of the Member Type categories**.

5. Produce a list of all of the customers' names for customers **who live in Helston Road**.

Portfolio items

Horror query based on **Video** table.

DVD query based on **Video** table.

Censor18 query based on **Video** table.

Old Vids query based on **Video** table.

Jurassic query based on **Video** table.

New Members query based on **Customer** table.

More advanced queries

Topic objectives

You can use more than one criterion in a query, and by doing this you can ask more detailed questions.

This topic shows you how to:

- use logic in queries
- change the priority of sorting records
- use queries to calculate simple summary information.

Examples of more detailed queries

We might want to find out various things using the data stored in a table. For example, some questions that might be asked about the **Video** table are:

- Which videos were purchased in May?
- Which videos cost between £5 and £10?
- Which videos have either a 12 or 15 certificate?
- Which videos have the word 'blue' in the title?
- Which videos are in the Action category and have a 15 certificate?
- Which videos are in the Action category *or* have a 15 certificate?
- Which videos are in the thriller category *or* are in DVD format?
- Which videos do not have PG or U censor ratings?

Some of these questions will allow us to explore the logic of AND and OR in a query.

Which videos were purchased in May?

This query requires a criterion that will select records with a Date of Acquisition that is between 1/5/01 AND 31/5/01. Chosen records have to satisfy both conditions, so this is known as AND logic, that is, both conditions must be true.

1. Create a new query using the **Video** table.

2. Add all the fields to the query.

3. In the criteria cell of the **Date of Acquisition** field, type *between 1/5/01 and 31/5/01*.

4. Click on the **DATASHEET** or **RUN QUERY** button. The resulting dynaset should only contain records of videos that were bought between the two dates. The criterion is inclusive, that is any record with either the start or the end date will be selected.

| Date of Acquisition |
| Video |
| |
| ☑ |
| Between #01/05/2001# And #31/05/2001# |

5. Return to the Design view and notice that Access puts hashes around dates. Save this query as *Purchases May 01*.

Which videos cost between £5 and £10?

1 With the previous query open, use **FILE-SAVE AS** to save the query as **Cost £5-£10**. Delete the criterion used for the previous query.

2 Continue in the query design view using the **Video** table, and use the criterion **Between 5 and 10** in the criteria row of the **Cost** field. Save the query and view the data.

Which videos have either a 12 or 15 certificate?

Records that satisfy this query have a censor rating of 12 OR a censor rating of 15. If either condition is true then the record is true – this is known as OR logic.

1 Use **FILE-SAVE AS** to save this query as **12-15 Rating**. Delete the criterion used for the previous query.

2 In the **criteria** cell of the **Censor Rating** field, type **12**. In the OR cell type **15**. Save the query.

3 Click on the **DATASHEET** or **RUN QUERY** button and view the resulting dynaset. Return to Design view.

Field:	Censor Rating
Table:	Video
Sort:	
Show:	☑
Criteria:	"12"
or:	15

Which videos have the word 'blue' in the title?

Text criteria may be entered using no quotes, single quotes, or double quotes. Access will convert a text criterion entered *without* quotes to be enclosed in double quotes. If you use one of the text criteria below, then typing **"*blue*"**, **'*blue*'**, or ***blue*** would produce the same result and Access would convert *blue* to "*blue*".

Text criterion	Finds
"T*"	text beginning with T
"*ing"	text ending with ing
"*b*"	text containing the letter b

1 Use **FILE-SAVE AS** to save this query as **Blue**. Delete thecriterion used for the previous query. In the criteria field of Title type ***blue***. Note that Access will convert this to read Like "*blue*".

Title
Video
☑
blue

2 Click on the **DATASHEET** or **RUN QUERY** button and view the resulting dynaset. Return to the Design view.

Which videos are in the Action category and have a 15 certificate?

This query uses AND logic, that is, any records selected need both criteria to be true.

1 Use **FILE-SAVE AS** to save this query as **Action and 15**. Delete the criterion used for the previous query. In the criteria field of **Video Category**, type **Action**. Note that Access will put quotes around this as you tab to the **Censor Rating** column. In the criteria row of **Censor Rating** type **15**.

Video Category	Censor Rating
Video	Video
☑	☑
"Action"	"15"

2 Click on the **DATASHEET** or **RUN QUERY** button and view the resulting dynaset. Return to the Design view.

Which videos are in the Action category *or* have a I5 certificate?

This query uses OR logic, that is, any records selected need one or other of the criteria to be true. You should find that more records are selected than in the last query.

1 Use **FILE-SAVE AS** to save this query as ***Action or 15***. Delete the criterion used for the previous query. In the criteria field of **Video Category**, type ***Action***. Note that Access will put quotes around this as you tab to the **Censor Rating** column. In the **or:** row of **Censor Rating** put ***15***.

Field:	Video Category	Censor Rating
Table:	Video	Video
Sort:		
Show:	☑	☑
Criteria:	"Action"	
or:		"15"

2 Click on the **DATASHEET** or **RUN QUERY** button and view the resulting dynaset. Return to the Design view.

Which videos are in the thriller category or are in DVD format?

This is another query that uses OR logic. Save this query as **Thriller or DVD**. Try the criteria shown below.

Field:	Censor Rating	Date of Acquisition	Format
Table:	Video	Video	Video
Sort:			
Show:	☑	☑	☑
Criteria:	"Thriller"		
or:			No

Run the query.

Which videos do not have PG or U censor ratings?

The mathematical operators introduced in the previous topic can be combined using AND and OR logic. To answer the query both 'Censor Rating not equal to PG' AND 'Censor Rating not equal to U' have to be true to omit these records from the dynaset.

Censor Rating
Video
☑
<>"PG" And <>"U"

Save this query as ***Not PG, U***. Run the query. Close the query.

Changing the order of fields in sorting queries

Using the sort row in the query grid allows you to sort records in a particular order, for example, by last name. You might wish to sort the records using more than one field. For example, after sorting records into last name order you might also like them to be in first name order (within last name, so that Mary Jones is before Peter Jones). The following exercise will investigate this.

1 Create a query based on the **Video** table and add the fields **Video Category**,

Censor Rating and **Title** in this order. Choose **ASCENDING** for the Sort order for the three fields.

Field:	Video Category	Censor Rating	Title
Table:	Video	Video	Video
Sort:	Ascending	Ascending	Ascending
Show:	☑	☑	☑
Criteria:			

2 View the resulting dynaset and note the order in which the records are displayed. Return to Design view and save the query as *Sort1*.

3 Highlight the **Censor Rating** field (click grey bar at top). Point to that bar area (point should change to an arrow) and click and drag so that this field is dropped into the left-most column. If this does not work you can delete all the fields and drag them on to the grid again in the order shown below. Use **FILE-SAVE AS** and save this query as *Sort2*.

Field:	Censor Rating	Video Category	Title
Table:	Video	Video	Video
Sort:	Ascending	Ascending	Ascending
Show:	☑	☑	☑
Criteria:			

4 View the resulting dynaset and note the difference between this result and the last. Close the query. You should see both **Sort1** and **Sort2** listed in the Database window.

52

Simple summary queries

As well as selecting and sorting, queries can be used to count records and total fields. The following exercise shows you how to design a query that will tell you how many videos there are in each category.

1 Create a query based on the **Video** table, add the field **Video Category** and then add this field again so you have two columns entitled Video Category.

2 Click on the **TOTALS** button in the toolbar and you will see an extra row added to the query grid. The default setting for this row is Group By. Open the drop-down list for the **Total** row of the second column and select **COUNT**.

Field:	Video Category	Video Category
Table:	Video	Video
Total:	Group By	Count
Sort:		Max
Show:	☑	Count
Criteria:		StDev
or:		Var
		First
		Last
		Expression
		Where

3 Run the query. It should now give you a list of the categories and the numbers of videos in each category. Save the query as *Category Count*.

Video Category	CountOfVideo
Action	6
Childrens	6
Comedy	13
Drama	13
Horror	6
Sci Fi	11
Thriller	10

4 Close this query. Create another query in a similar manner using the field **Censor Rating** to count how many videos are in each rating. Save the query as *Censor Rating Count* and close it.

5 Open the query **Category Count** in Design view and use **FILE-SAVE AS** to save it as *Category Totals*. Drag the **Cost** field to the grid and choose **SUM** in the **TOTAL** row for this field. When you run this query you should see the total cost for each category. Close the query.

Field:	Video Category	Video Category	Cost
Table:	Video	Video	Video
Total:	Group By	Count	Sum
Sort:			
Show:	☑	☑	☑
Criteria:			

Queries using the *Customer* table

The following queries require the use of the logical query operators, AND and OR. Create queries using the **Customer** table that show all of the fields and answer the following questions:

1 Which customers live in Halwyn Bay or joined after 1/5/01?

2 Which customers joined in the last six months of 2000?

The following queries require the use of sorting:

3 List the names and addresses of customers in last name then first name order.

4 List the names of customers in Membership Category then Date Joined order.

The following query is a totals query:

5 How many customers are there in each Membership category?

Portfolio items

Queries: **Purchases May 01, Cost £5-£10, 12-15 Rating, Blue, Action and 15, Action or 15, Not PG, U.**

Sort1, Sort2 queries.

Category Count query.

Censor Rating Count query.

Category Totals query.

Screen forms

Topic objectives

A screen form is a more user-friendly way than the basic datasheet (introduced in Topic 5) in which to work with your data. Screen forms can be used to enter, edit and display data on screen. Different screen forms are designed for different purposes, and a complex database system may have many screen forms.

This topic shows you how to:

- create a form using AutoForm
- create a form using Form Wizard
- save a form
- use a form
- print a form.

Understanding the purpose of screen forms

In Topic 5 you entered data into tables using the Datasheet view of the table. This is a 'quick and dirty' way of entering data into a database. The disadvantage of using the Datasheet view is that the fields in a record often do not all fit on the screen. Also, viewing and entering data in the datasheet grid can be somewhat tiresome. Such an approach to data entry would certainly not be suitable for a customer registration form for an e-merchant. Customers and employees creating databases need a data entry format that prompts them regarding the data that they are expected to enter, and offers boxes for data entry in a sequence that follows a natural 'dialog' on the screen.

Data is often collected manually customers or employees filling out a form. In a form there are boxes to fill in with, for example, name and address, and there may be boxes that are ticked, for example Yes/No boxes. On-screen forms seek to replicate and even improve upon these paper-based forms. Typically, text fields in a form have a label and a box into which text can be entered. A Yes/No field has a tick box that can be clicked On or Off. On more sophisticated forms where perhaps a field can only take one of a number of values (says specific categories of videos), these categories may be displayed in a drop-down box next to the text box. The user can click on the appropriate category in the drop-down list to enter it into the text box.

Complex database applications need at least one form for each table in the database, but sometimes there will be additional forms to support the editing of data in specific fields. Standard forms are created for most applications or jobs, for example, a form for entering the details of a new customer or video.

Forms can be used to enter, edit, display and print data contained in your tables. They offer the advantage of presenting data, on screen, in an organised and attractive manner.

The easiest way to create a form with Access is to use AutoForm. If you want more choice in the fields that are added to the form, and the form format or style, Form Wizard is a straightforward, but slightly more flexible, approach to form creation. These are the two approaches that will be explored in this unit. Access also provides a range of tools for customising forms for specific applications. It is possible to move fields around forms, format text of labels, add lines and rectangles, and insert a range of objects such as images (say for a logo). If you want to explore some of these more advanced features you should consult the companion book to this one – *Access 2000 An Advanced Course for Students*.

Using AutoForm to create a Columnar form

There are three types of form that can be created using AutoForm:

- Columnar
- Tabular
- Datasheet.

In this activity we explore the creation of a Columnar form. Later activities show other types of form. A Columnar form displays data one record at a time. Tabular and Datasheet forms both display more than one record at once. If there are a lot of fields in the records then the entire record will not fit on the screen, and it will be necessary to scroll to view the full record.

AutoForm creates a form instantly using all fields in the records of the underlying table. To create a form for the **Video** database using AutoForm:

55

1 Starting from the Database window, click on **FORMS** in the **Objects** column and then click on the **NEW** button to display the **NEW FORM** dialog box.

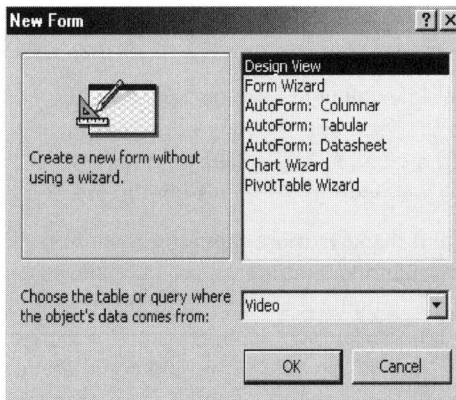

FIGURE 11.1

2 Click on the list box button of the **CHOOSE THE TABLE OR QUERY WHERE THE OBJECT'S DATA COMES FROM** box, to produce a list of tables and queries and select the **Video** table.

3 Select the **AUTOFORM:COLUMNAR** option and click on **OK**.

4 Choose **FILE-SAVE**, or click on the **SAVE** button and give the form the name *VideoCol*.

(5) Close the form using **FILE-CLOSE** or the **CLOSE** button of the form window.

Saving, closing and opening a form

Forms can be saved by choosing **FILE-SAVE** or clicking on the **SAVE** button. With new forms, which have not previously been saved, Access will prompt for a file name with a **FILE SAVE AS** dialog box. Also, if you wish later to save an existing form with a different name (perhaps so that you have different versions of the form on which you are working), then **FILE-SAVE AS** can be used and an alternative name for the form entered in the dialog box.

It is important to be clear that the name and title of a form are not the same thing (even if you used the same label or words). The name and title have different functions. The form title is displayed at the top of the form window. The name you give when saving the form is the form's file or object name, which you need to be able to recognise when you want to open the form for use again. These names appear when the **FORMS** object is selected in the database window.

To **close** a form use **FILE-CLOSE** or click on the **CLOSE** button of the form window. If the form or the latest modification has not been saved you will be prompted to save. When a form is closed, its name (the one you gave to it when saving) will be shown in the database window when you select the **FORMS** object.

To **open** a form from the Database window, click on **FORMS** in the object list, select the name of the form required and click on the **OPEN** button.

Using Form Wizard to create a Tabular form

Form Wizard allows more flexibility in form design than AutoForm. For example, the fields to be included in the form and the look of the form can be selected. In addition, Form Wizard supports the creation of justified forms, as well as Columnar, Tabular and Datasheet forms. A justified form displays one record at a time in a row format.

A Tabular form is one that displays more than one record on the screen. The field names form headers for columns, and the records are shown below them in a table, as shown in Figure 11.2. The number of records displayed will depend upon the size of the window and the number of records in the table. If there are a lot of fields in a record it is unlikely that you will be able to see the complete record on the screen and you will need to scroll to the right to display more of the fields. This type of form is suited to records with only a few fields. The advantage of this form is that it displays more than one record at a time, and makes it easier to scan parts of a small database.

To create a Tabular form for the **Video** table:

(1) First close any open form.

(2) From the Database window with the **FORMS** object selected click on **NEW**.

③ In the **NEW FORM** drop-down list box, select the **Video** table.

④ Select **FORMWIZARD** and click on **OK**.

⑤ Add all the fields to the form and click on the **NEXT>** button (see below for guidance on adding fields to the form).

⑥ Choose a **TABULAR** form and click on the **NEXT>** button.

⑦ Next choose the look for your form from the standard looks that are available and click on **NEXT>**.

⑧ Enter the title for the form as *Videos Available for Loan*. Click on the **FINISH** button to display the form.

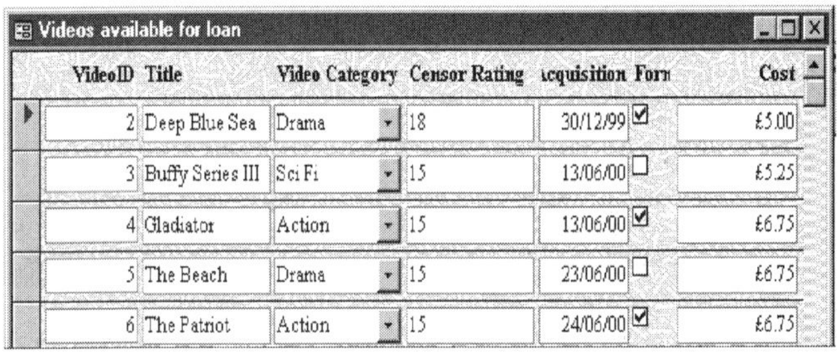

FIGURE 11.2

The difference between this form and the single column form is that the fields are arranged in columns. The top of the column is headed by the field name. Note that the Wizard has not displayed all the field names properly. You will see how to improve this in Topic 14. The data displayed will be the data already entered into the **Video** table in earlier units. If you had not entered any data into the underlying table, the form would be blank, but would still show the field names at the top of each column.

57

⑨ Save the form as *VideoTab*. Close the form.

Selecting fields for forms

As discussed above, when using Form Wizard you need to select the fields that will be feature on the form. At the appropriate stage in the Form Wizard dialog, the fields that you can have in the form are shown in the **AVAILABLE FIELDS** box.

These can be transferred to the **SELECTED FIELDS** box by means of selecting each field in turn and clicking on the > button.

If you wish to add all the fields in the table to the form then click on the >> button.

You may set the order in which the fields appear on the form by selecting them in the order you desire. The < button will remove a highlighted field from a form and << will remove all the fields from the form.

Once you have added the required fields to the form, continue by clicking on the **NEXT>** button.

Using Form Wizard to create a Columnar form

The previous exercises have created two different kinds of forms to support data entry and display for the **Video** table. This activity asks you to follow through similar steps to those above, and to use Form Wizard to create a Columnar form for the **Customer** table. This form should allow data entry into all of the fields in the **Customer** table. This form will be used next to add more data to the **Customer** table. Save the form as *CustomersCol*.

Using Form Wizard to create a Justified form

Next create another form for use with the **Customer** table. This form should be designed to display customer data on the screen that might be useful when videos are being returned or checked out. You may use your own title, and make your own decisions about which fields to include. Save this form as *CustomersJus*. Is this the best type of form for this application?

Using a form to enter data into the *Customer* table

To use a form, first display the available forms in the Database window by clicking on the **FORM** button in that window. Open the form either by selecting it and clicking on **OPEN** or by double-clicking on its name.

You can use the form to look at the data in the table (or query) upon which it is based. Whether it is a single column or Tabular form, use the record movement keys in the status bar or use the **EDIT-GO TO** menu to move around the records in your form. Using the **PAGE UP** and **PAGE DOWN** keys with a single column form will display the next/previous record, whereas with a Tabular form they will either page up or page down a screenful of records.

To enter new records using a form:

1 Open **CustomersCol**.

2 If there are already records in the table, go to the end of your records using the new record button on the status bar or the toolbar.

3 Using the data in Appendix 1, enter the next ten records for the **Customer** table. Enter data into each record in turn by filling in the boxes for each field. When you have completed each text box (control) press **ENTER** or **TAB** to move to the next one.

4 Close the form when you have finished entering the data.

Printing forms

Forms, as opposed to reports, are designed primarily for screen use, i.e. they are intended for data to be entered via the computer and they display the data on screen. However, Access offers the facility to print from a form. Before printing a form always preview it first. A form can be previewed from either the Run or Design view mode.

To print the **CustomersCol** form:

1 Open the **CustomersCol** form.

2 Click on the **PRINT PREVIEW** button in the toolbar, and a miniature version of what is to be printed will be displayed.

3 To zoom-in and zoom-out simply click anywhere on the preview, or use the **ZOOM** button. Clicking on the right mouse button will allow you to select the degree of magnification.

4 Use **FILE-PAGE SETUP** and/or **FILE-PRINT** to make adjustments such as the orientation, portrait or landscape, the choice of printer, the width of the margins, and the pages to be printed. If no adjustments are necessary, then click on the **PRINT** button.

5 Close the form.

Portfolio items

VideoCol screen form (created using AutoForm).

VideoTab screen form (created using Form Wizard).

CustomersCol screen form.

CustomersJus screen form.

Reports

Topic objectives

Reports are designed to support the display or printing of data in a table or set of tables. This topic explores the basic design of reports. Although the basic reports that will be explored in this unit will display or print all of the data in your small trial database, in real applications, reports allow printing of selected records or fields in the table. Topic 14 shows how the records to be included in a report can be selected, through the use of queries.

This topic shows you how to:

- create a report using AutoReport
- create a report using Report Wizard
- save and close a report
- use a report
- print a report.

Understanding the purpose of reports

Reports are used to print information from a number of records. Reports can show the data from either a table or a query. In addition to records, reports may include summary information relating to the records.

Reports, then, are intended to allow you to select the data to be printed and then to present that data in an acceptable format. The distinction between reports and forms – which students often find difficult – is becoming ever more blurred. The traditional position is that screen forms were for data entry and on-screen display of data. Reports are concerned with output from the database, and are typically printed. However, with the increase in electronic documents, reports may also be compiled into an electronic document that can be viewed on screen. Screen forms can be used to display individual records, during transactions with customers, and the facilities often also exist for printing them. To really be able to differentiate between forms and reports it is useful to look at and compare their respective formatting options in a database package such as Access. The distinction can also be made in specific applications. With the Halwyn Videos database, screen forms may be used to:

- Input data into the **Video** table as new videos are added.
- Input data into the **Customer** table as new customers join.
- Change records in either of the above tables when, for example, a customer moves address.
- Delete records from each of the above tables when customers or videos have been inactive for some months.
- Check details of individual customers on screen during in-shop transactions.

Reports, on the other hand, may be used to:

- Create a mailing list of customers.
- List the new videos added to the stock during the last six months.
- Create a list of members in a specific category – perhaps all of those in the Childrens category.
- Undertake an evaluation of the value of the current stock of videos.
- Create a ranking of the top ten selling videos in the last week (this also needs transaction data that has not been entered into either of our tables to date).

As illustrated above, most applications have a number of different standard reports.

The easiest way to create a report with Access is to use AutoReport. If you want more choice in the fields that are added to the report, and the report format or style, Report Wizard is a straightforward, but slightly more flexible approach to report creation. These are the two approaches that will be explored in this topic. Access also provides a range of tools for customising reports for specific applications. It is possible to move fields around reports, format text of labels, add lines and rectangles, and insert a range of objects such as images (say for a logo). If you want to explore some of these more advanced features you should consult the companion book to this: *Access 2000 An Advanced Course for Students*.

Since forms and reports share many design and creation features, you will re-use some of the skills that you acquired earlier in designing a form to help you to design a report.

Using AutoReport to create a Columnar report

The really easy way to create a report is to allow Access to do all of the work for you, by using AutoReport.

AutoReport creates two different types of report:

- Columnar
- Tabular.

In this activity we explore the creation of a Columnar report. A columnar report displays data one record at a time. For many uses of reports this is too lengthy, and the summary formats of Tabular and other report forms are preferred. AutoReport creates a report instantly using all fields in the records of the underlying table. This, however, does not allow the specification of the order of records in the report or the style of the report.

To use AutoReport to create a columnar report for the **Video** table:

1 Starting from the Database window, select **REPORTS** in the Objects column and then click on the **NEW** button.

2 Click on the list box button of the **CHOOSE THE TABLE OR QUERY WHERE THE OBJECT'S DATA**

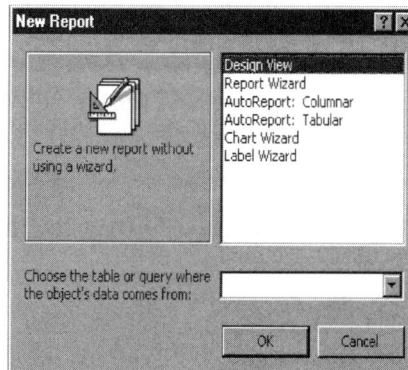

FIGURE 12.1

COMES FROM box, to produce a list of tables and queries and select the **Video** table.

3 Select the **AUTOREPORT: COLUMNAR** option.

4 Click on **OK** and the report will be created and displayed on the screen.

5 Choose **FILE-SAVE**, or click on the **SAVE** button and give the report the name *VideoColR*.

Note: The above exercise has created a parallel report to the form created in Topic 11 with AutoForm. Both reports are in Columnar format. What are the similarities and differences between these two documents?

Notes on saving, closing and opening a report

Reports can be saved by choosing **FILE-SAVE** or clicking on the **SAVE** button. With new reports, which have not previously been saved, Access will prompt for a file name with a **FILE SAVE AS** dialog box. Also, if you wish later to save an existing report with a different name (perhaps so that you have different versions of the report on which you are working), then **FILE-SAVE AS** can be used and an alternative name for the report entered in the dialog box.

It is important to be clear that the name and title of a report are not the same thing (even if you used the same label or words). The name and title have different functions. The report title is displayed at the top of the report. The name you give when saving the report is the report's file or object name, which you need to be able to recognise when you want to open the report for use again. These names appear in the Database window when **REPORTS** is the object selected. Reports are opened and closed in the same manner as forms.

62

Using Report Wizard to create a Single Column report

There are various types of report that can be created with a Report Wizard. First we deal with the Single Column report, which is used most frequently and is relatively simple to create. A Single Column report places all of the selected fields in a single column, with their field names to the left, as shown in Figure 12.4. This type of report displays more than one record at a time, and makes it easier to scan a list of the records in a small database. The Report Wizard is different from the AutoReport because it allows you to select which fields are to be used in the report.

To create a Tabular form report for the **Video** table:

1 From the Database window with the **REPORTS** object selected, click on the **NEW** button.

2 In the **NEW REPORT** dialog box select the **Video** table.

3 Select **REPORT WIZARD** option and click on **OK**.

4 The next stage is to choose which fields are to be in the report. The fields that you can have in the report are shown in the **AVAILABLE FIELDS** box. For this report we want to include the following fields: **VideoID**, **Title**, **Category**, and **Date of Acquisition**.

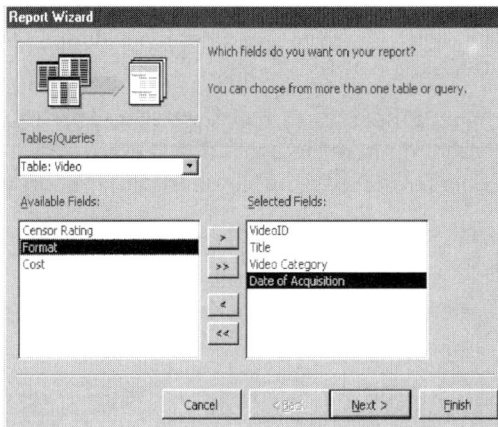

FIGURE 12.2

5 Transfer the fields required to the report by selecting each field in turn and clicking on the > button. If you wish to add all the fields in the table to the report then click on the >> button. You may set the order in which the fields appear on the report by selecting them in the order that you desire. The < button will remove a highlighted field from a report and << will remove all the fields from the report.

6 Once you have added the required fields to the report continue by clicking on the **NEXT>** button.

7 The next dialog box asks you to indicate grouping levels. Leave this for now by clicking on the **NEXT>** button.

8 Now attention turns to the sort order of the records. Select the **Date of Acquisition** as the field that you want the records to be sorted by. Since you have only a small set of records, just one sort field will be adequate. If you want records to appear in the same order as in the table or query it is not necessary to indicate a sort field. Choose the **NEXT>** button.

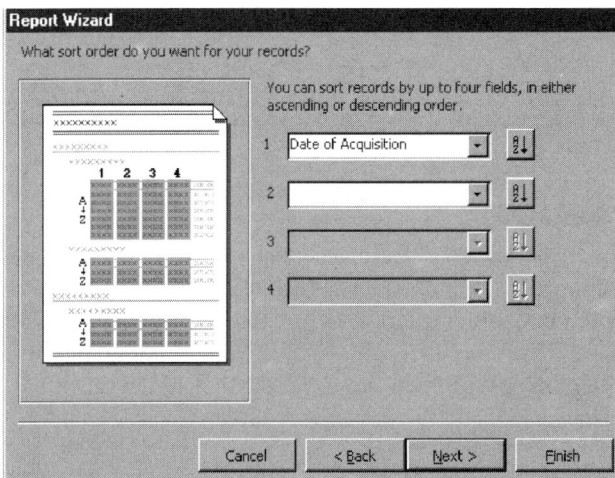

FIGURE 12.3

⑨ Next we turn to the layout of the printout on the paper and whether the report is to be in portrait or landscape orientation. Choose **COLUMNAR** and **PORTRAIT**. Click on the **NEXT>** button.

⑩ There is a choice of style for the report: Bold/Casual/Compact/Corporate/ Formal/Soft Gray. The style decides the appearance of the field names and field contents in the report. An example of the style is shown on the left of the dialog box. Click on each style in turn to see what it would look like. Choose **CORPORATE**. The style can be modified later. Click on the **NEXT>** button.

⑪ Enter a report title as *Videos Listed by Date of Acquisition*. Note that report titles are particularly important in signalling the purpose and contents of the report to the reader. This is also the name that the report is saved with.

⑫ With the option **PREVIEW THE REPORT** selected, click on the **FINISH** button to display the report.

⑬ Examine the report and its format. Note that Access has added a page number and the date at the bottom of every page.

Videos Listed by Date of Acquisition

FIGURE 12.4

Date of Acquisition	30/12/99
VideoID	2
Title	Deep Blue Sea
Video Category	Drama

64

Using Report Wizard to create a report for the *Customer* table

The previous exercises have created two different kinds of reports to support the creation of printed reports of the data in the **Video** database. This activity asks you to follow through the similar steps to those above, and to use Report Wizard to create a report for the **Customer** table. This report should allow printing and formatting of all of the data in the Customer table. Choose your own style and sort order. Save the report as *CustomersRep*.

Using a report

Once a report has been designed it is available as a format for displaying the data in the database. If the data in the database or query has been amended or extended, the report will show the new data. To use a report, first display the available report names in the Database window, then double-click on the report name and the **PRINT PREVIEW** window will appear showing a preview of how the report will appear when printed. Alternatively, click on the report name and then click on the **PREVIEW** button.

To zoom in and out and to view a complete page on the screen, click on the report.

Note: A report picks up the table properties of the table or query the report used when it was designed. If you subsequently change the properties of the table or query, this does not automatically change the properties of the report. In other words, in order to avoid confusion it is a good idea to be sure about the table and query definitions before you design reports.

Printing the *CustomersRep* report

To print the **CustomersRep** report:

1. Open the **CustomersRep** report.

2. Click on the **PRINT PREVIEW** button in the toolbar, and a miniature version of what is to be printed will be displayed.

3. To zoom-in and zoom-out simply click anywhere on the preview, or use the **ZOOM** button. Clicking on the right mouse button will allow you to select the degree of magnification.

4. Use **FILE-PAGE SETUP** to make adjustments such as the orientation (portrait or landscape), the choice of printer, and the width of the margins.

5. To print the report, click the **PRINT** button, or choose **FILE-PRINT**. If you want to print only selected pages, use **FILE-PRINT** and specify the pages required in the Print range section.

6. Close the preview.

Portfolio items

VideoColR, a column report for the **Video** table.

Videos Listed by Date of Acquisition, a tabular report for the **Video** table.

CustomersRep, a report for the **Customer** table.

Mailing reports and queries

Topic objectives

This topic focuses on two key interlinked themes: mailing label reports and queries. Mailing label reports are a special type of report that allow the creation of mailing labels, from, say, a table of names and addresses. A mailing label report fits the fields you select into a rectangle that is designed to print labels. Unlike other Report Wizard reports, this type does not show field names. It does, however, make it easy to add text such as commas and spaces. Often businesses do not want to mail all of the names on their databases, but prefer to select a subset with specific characteristics. This means using a query as the basis for the mailing label report.

This topic shows you how to:

- create a mailing label report
- use a query in the process of creating a Report Wizard report
- perform a mail merge to create an accompanying letter.

Creating a mailing label report, using a query

Mailing labels can be created for an entire database, and with your small database this would not be particularly onerous. However, in order to simulate a real life application, the mailing label report that is created here uses a query to select a subset of the database as its basis. Later you will use the same query to select the records for mail merge, to create the letters to go into the envelopes that will be labelled with the mailing labels.

You are asked to create a mailing label report that lists all members who have been in membership for more than a year. An extract from such a report is shown in Figure 13.1. First we need to define and execute a query to select the appropriate records, and then we need to define the mailing label report that is to be used to display this set of records.

Mrs Linda Ashleigh	Ms Freda Badock	Mr Robert Banks
Withney Court Farm	6 High Street	7 Horncroft Lane
Withney	Halwyn Bay	Halwyn Bay
Cornwall HE9 9FJ	Cornwall HE1 8YV	Cornwall HE6 3DR

FIGURE 13.1

Query design and execution were introduced in Topics 8, 9 and 10, and you may wish to review them at this point.

The procedure for creating a mailing label report is similar to that for creating any other type of report, except that you use a special Label Wizard.

We start by creating the query and then proceed to create the mailing label report with which we use the query:

1 Starting from the Database window, select the **QUERIES** object, and click on the **NEW** button to create a new query.

2 Choose **DESIGN VIEW** and click on **OK**.

3 The **SHOW TABLE** dialog box appears. Select the table **Customer** and click on the **ADD** button and then click on the **CLOSE** button.

4 Next choose to include all fields in the query by double-clicking on the title bar of the field list box of the table in the upper section of the window. Click anywhere in the selected area and drag to the field row to transfer all of the fields to the lower section.

5 In the **Date of Joining** criteria cell, enter the query criteria **<1/1/02**.

6 To view the result of this query, click on the **QUERY VIEW** button on the toolbar.

7 Save the query by choosing **FILE-SAVE**.

8 In the **QUERY NAME** box of the **SAVE AS** dialog box, enter the query name: *Loyal Customers*.

9 Close the query.

Now that you have defined a query, you need to design a report to display the records retrieved by the query.

10 Click on the **REPORTS** tab in the Database window and click on **NEW**.

11 Select the **LABEL WIZARD** option to create a report using Label Wizard.

12 From the **CHOOSE THE TABLE OR QUERY...** drop-down list, box select the query **Loyal Customers**. Click on **OK**.

13 Select the size of the labels. You may need to experiment with different label sizes. Try the first in the Avery list. Click on the **NEXT>** button.

67

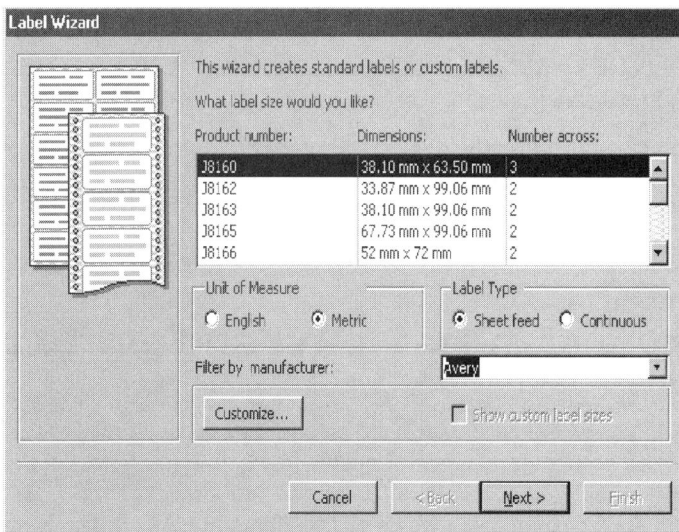

FIGURE 13.2

14 Select the font name, font size, font weight and text colour of your choice. Best to accept the settings given and click on the **NEXT>** button.

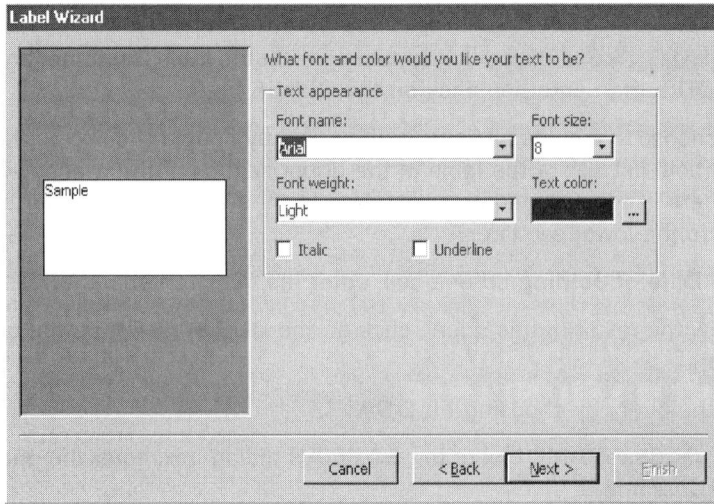

FIGURE 13.3

15) Add the field **Title** followed by a space and then the fields **First Name** and **Last Name** to the first line. Click on the **ENTER** button to move onto the next line.

16) Add **Street** to the next line.

17) Add the remainder of the fields, each to a separate line, with the exception of **County** and **Post Code**, which should be on the same line separated by a comma and a space. Click on the **NEXT>** button.

18) Choose to order the records in alphabetical order according to **Last Name**. Click on the **NEXT>** button.

Prototype label:

{Title} {First Name} {Last Name}
{Street}
{Town}
{County} {Post Code}

19) Accept the title **Labels Loyal Customers**. The report is automatically saved.

20) With **SEE THE LABELS AS THEY WILL LOOK PRINTED** selected, click on **FINISH** to display the report on the screen.

21) To print the report directly, click on the **PRINT** button. To display the **PRINT** dialog box use **FILE-PRINT**.

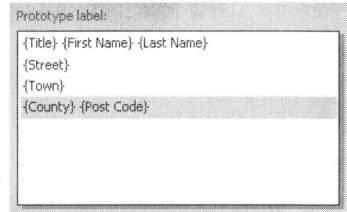

Creating a standard letter and performing a mail merge

For this activity you will need to use Word as well as Access. A mail merge requires two things; a source of data (e.g. list of people to whom personalised letters will be sent) and a 'standard' letter. This letter contains text that will be the same for each letter and also 'replaceable' fields which will be different for each letter, as they will use the data list to retrieve the approprite text. The **Loyal Customers** query created above will be used as a data source for the following mail merge.

1) Close the query you have just created (**Loyal Customers**). You should have the **QUERIES** object selected in the objects list and will see **Loyal Customers** in the list of queries.

2 Highlight this query and click on the **OFFICE LINKS** button. This will display a drop-down list. Choose the **MERGE IT WITH MS WORD** option.

Merge It with MS Word
Publish It with MS Word
Analyze It with MS Excel

3 The Word Mail Merge Wizard starts and the following dialog box is displayed. Choose the option to **CREATE A NEW DOCUMENT AND THEN LINK THE DATA TO IT**.

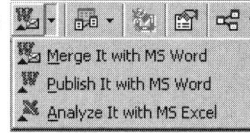

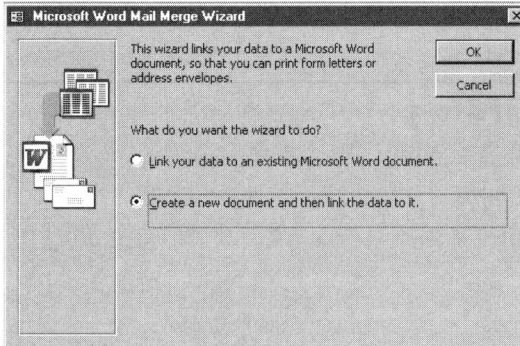

Microsoft Word Mail Merge Wizard

This wizard links your data to a Microsoft Word document, so that you can print form letters or address envelopes.

OK
Cancel

What do you want the wizard to do?

○ Link your data to an existing Microsoft Word document.

◉ Create a new document and then link the data to it.

FIGURE 13.4

4 Word starts and displays a new document. If this document 'disappears' you can redisplay it by clicking on its button on the toolbar. Notice, though, that there is a Mail Merging toolbar.

5 Key in the name and address of Halwyn Videos (see Figure 13.5). If you wish you may add some clip art to give the letter more impact. You can also select a suitable font.

6 Click on the **INSERT MERGE FIELD BUTTON** and you will see a list of fields available to you. Your list may not be exactly as the one illustrated. The fields required for the mail merge are the same as those for the label, i.e. **Title**, **First Name**, **Last Name**, **Street**, **Town**, **County** and **Post Code**.

Insert Merge Field ▾ Insert
CustomerID
First_Name
Last_Name
Title
Street
Town
County
Post_Code
Customer_Category
Date_Joined
Gender

69

7 Create the customer's address by building up their name and address using the merge fields. Add the salutation line and your letter should look like the one illustrated.

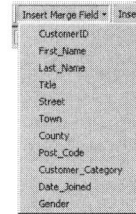

Halwyn Videos
The Promenade
Halwyn Bay
Cornwall
HE6 5EB

12/12/01

«Title» «First_Name» «Last_Name»
«Street»
«Town»
«County» «Post_Code»

FIGURE 13.5

Dear «Title» «Last_Name»

As a loyal customer please find enclosed a full-price rental voucher. We pride ourselves on being able to offer a selection of the latest films and hope we can continue to provide you with many hours of enjoyable viewing.

Yours sincerely

Peter Merryfield
Manager

8 Add the text as illustrated and save the document as *Loyal Customers*.

9 It is best to check the merge for errors first. Do this by clicking on the **CHECK FOR ERRORS** button. If you do have any problems, a merge field can be deleted by highlighting it and pressing the **DELETE** key. You may then print the merged document or click on the **MERGE TO NEW DOCUMENT** button for an electronic copyl. Close the document and close Word.

Portfolio items

Loyal Customers query.

Labels Loyal Customers report.

Loyal Customers mail merge letter.

More on forms

Topic objectives

Topic 11 showed you how to create simple forms using AutoForm and Form Wizard. Whilst this is a good way to get started, systems designers will often want to create forms to their own design. In order to do this it is important to understand a little more about the underlying structure of forms. Forms are constructed from a collection of individual design elements, which are called *controls*. The controls that appear on the forms created so far are:

- labels, so that you know what each part of the form is for
- text boxes, for entering data.

This topic shows you how to:

- display the form customising tools, including the toolbox, palette, properties and field list
- move and size controls
- align controls
- add text to a form.

Many of the concepts and tools that are introduced in this topic also apply to reports. We shall explore the customisation of reports in the next topic. Neither this topic nor Topic 15 aim to make you an expert at form or report design. They are intended to give you some insights into the processes associated with form and report design.

Components of a form

Forms are comprised of a number of components, as named and described in the table below. In a form created with Form Wizard, only the form header band and the detail band contain controls. The header band contains information that will always appear at the top of the form, usually the title of the form. The detail band contains the controls for displaying the data.

Component	Function
Form Header	Contains text such as the form's title, but field headers and graphics may also be put into a header section.
Detail	Contains the controls (field labels, text boxes and check boxes) that display data from your table for which the form has been designed.
Form Footer	Similar in function to the Form Header and may contain information such as the date.

Right Margin	The position of the right margin is indicated by a vertical line on the right edge of the form. This right margin can be moved by clicking and dragging it.
Bottom Margin	A horizontal line that indicates the bottom margin of the form. This can also be positioned by clicking and dragging.
Scroll Bars	Vertical and horizontal scroll bars enable you to move the form within its window.

Using Form Design view

So far in this series of units, a form has only been opened in Form Run or Data view. This is the mode in which forms are usually run where they display and – more importantly – accept data. A form can also be shown in Design view, which allows modifications to be made to its layout. In Design view, data cannot be entered into the form, only the layout and appearance of the form can be changed.

To open the **VideoCol** from in Form Design view:

1. From the Database window, click on the **FORM** tab.

2. Select the **VideoCol** form and click on the **DESIGN** button.

Once a form is open you may switch between the Form Run (Data) view and the Design view by clicking on the **VIEW** button on the toolbar.

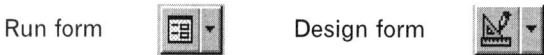

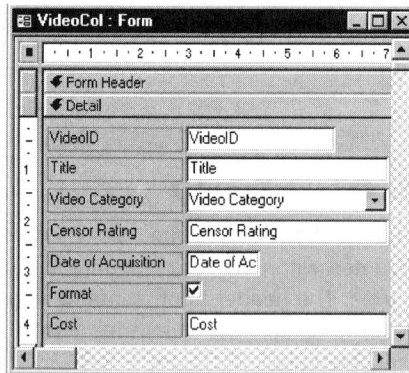

Run form   Design form

FIGURE 14.1

Features of Design view

1. In Design view, instead of data appearing in the controls, the field names appear. Text or controls may be selected and moved to achieve the layout desired.

2. A field usually has two controls, a **label control** in which the field name appears and a **text box control** in which the data will appear when the form is run.

3. Other features of design mode are:

- availability of rulers and grid
- design aids in the form of other small windows
- the **Toolbox**
- the **Field List**
- the **Properties Sheet**.

4 The **Toolbox** offers a selection of tools by which controls and text may be added to the form. The **Field List** shows a list of fields in the table that the form was based upon and the **Properties Sheet** is a list of properties. The list of properties will depend upon what part of the form is selected. You will become familiar with these as you progress through the tasks.

To display the **Toolbox**, click on the **TOOLBOX** button or use **VIEW-TOOLBOX**. To display the **Field List** click on the **FIELD LIST** button or choose **VIEW-FIELD LIST**. To display the **Properties Sheet** click on the **PROPERTIES** button on the toolbar or choose **VIEW-PROPERTIES**.

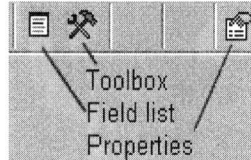

Toolbox
Field list
Properties

5 Colour selection can be made using the drop-down buttons on the formatting toolbar.

Customising a form

The easiest way to learn about customising a form is to experiment. Therefore this topic does not give you step-by-step instructions, but rather sets you the task of developing the form in Figure 14.2. In order to create this form you will need to:

- Move and size the controls.
- Select groups of controls.
- Alter the size and font of controls.
- Change the area of some sections of the form.
- Add text to the form.

We suggest that you work through these activities in the order specified above. Guidance on how to perform the various operations is given below. Start with **VideoCol**, and use **FILE-SAVE AS** to save it as **_VideoEntry_** and switch to Design view.

FIGURE 14.2

73

Moving and sizing controls

Before you can move or size a control you must click on it to select it. When selected, the control is enclosed by an outlining rectangle, with an anchor rectangle at its upper left corner and five smaller rectangles. These smaller rectangles are sizing handles. On Columnar forms, text boxes often have associated labels and when you select one of these objects they are both selected together as a unit.

To	Do this
Select a text box control and its label (if it has a label)	Click anywhere on either the label or the text box.
Move a text box control and its label (if it has a label)	Move the pointer over the text box control or its label until it changes to a hand. Click and drag the label and text box to new position.
Move label or text box control separately	Point to the anchor handle at the top left corner of either the label or text box control, until it changes to the shape of a pointing hand. Click and drag to new position.
Adjust the width and height of a control simultaneously	Point to one of the small sizing handles at one of the three corners, until it changes to a diagonal two-headed arrow. Click and drag to size required.
Adjust only the height (or width) of the control	Point to one of the sizing handles on the horizontal (or vertical) edge of the outline, until it changes to a vertical two-headed arrow. Click and drag to height (or width) required.
Automatically adjust label or control to fit to text	Double-click one of the sizing handles.

Selecting and moving a group of controls

Selecting and moving a group of controls is useful if you want to keep the relative spacing of a group of objects yet want to move them to another part of the form.

To select a group of objects:

- Imagine that the group of objects is enclosed by a rectangle. Use the pointer and by clicking and dragging draw this rectangle on the form. When you release the mouse button all the objects within this rectangle will be selected.
- Alternatively, select one object and hold down the SHIFT key whilst selecting the next and subsequent objects.
- If the group of controls is in a horizontal or vertical line, click on the ruler at the place where the 'line' would cross.

To move the whole group, point to any of the controls and with pointer as the shape of a hand drag the group to a new position.

To move an individual control in the group, point to its anchor handle and drag.

To deselect the whole group, click anywhere outside the selected area.

Using the ruler and the grid

VIEW-RULER allows you to choose whether the ruler is displayed. Rulers aid in the positioning of controls. **VIEW-GRID** will display or hide a grid, which also aids the positioning of controls.

Altering the size and font of controls

To alter the size or font of controls in a form:

1 Select the control(s) to be altered.

2 Open the **FONT** list box in the toolbar and select the font required.

3 Open the **FONT SIZE** list box and select the point size required.

4 Click on the left, centre or right alignment button in the toolbar.

Note: if you increase the size of a font you may need to alter the size of the control and the size of the section. Double-click a sizing handle for an automatic fit to text size.

Aligning a group of controls

Once you start to move controls around the form they can become untidy as they become misaligned. You can select labels and text boxes separately for alignment purposes. Click each text box and/or label while holding down the **SHIFT** key.

To	Do this
Align controls to the left or right	Choose **FORMAT-ALIGN-LEFT** or **FORMAT-ALIGN-RIGHT**.
Align controls to the top or bottom	Choose **FORMAT-ALIGN-TOP** or **FORMAT-ALIGN-BOTTOM**.
Align controls to the grid	Choose **FORMAT-ALIGN-TO GRID**.

Changing the form's area

The area of each section of a form, the header, detail and footer sections may be altered individually. Also the position of the right and bottom edge of a form may be adjusted. To alter the depth of a section of the form:

1 Move the pointer to the bottom edge of the section where it will change shape.

2 Drag down to increase the depth of the section.

To alter the area of the form, drag the right and bottom edges to the size that you require. Point to between **Form Header** and **Detail** and drag down to make space in the header section for a title.

Adding additional text

Additional text can be added to the form, such as a title in the form header or instructions regarding a tick box. Also you may edit the text of a field name label if required.

To	Do this
Add a label	Click on the **LABEL** tool in the Toolbox window, click on the form in the required position and type the text required. *Aa* Apply formatting (font, size, colour) as required.
Edit a label	Click on the label to select it, then click on it again to display an insertion point in the text. Edit the text as required. Press `ENTER` or click on a blank part of the form when finished.

Deleting fields from or restoring fields to a form

Note: If you delete a field you won't be able to use the form to enter data into this field. Use **EDIT-UNDO** if you unintentionally delete a field.

To	Do this
Delete a label or label and text box	Select the control and press `DELETE` or use **EDIT-DELETE** to delete both label and entry box. To delete only the label click on it again before deleting.
Restoring a label and field	Use **VIEW-FIELD LIST** to display the list of fields available in the table. Click on the field name required, and drag to required position on the form. If the form is a single column form then both label and field will appear, although the label will require editing. If the form is a tabular one then just the field will be restored.

Using the customised form to enter data

To gain a full appreciation of the modifications made to the **VideoEntry** form you need to use it to enter data.

1 Open the form from the Database window by clicking on the **OPEN** button.

2 Click on the **NEW RECORD** button to display a blank form.

3 Make up data for a new video and, using the form, enter the data into the next record.

4 Close the form.

Creating your own form for *Customer* data entry

Your task here is to create a form for data entry into the **Customer** table. Figure 14.3 shows a form that should give you some ideas. You can use some of the processes described above in your form design. Organise the form in a way that you feel is appropriate for how you are going to use it. Apply formatting, such as fonts, that is consistent with your house style. Save your form as *CustomerEntry*.

Tip: If you add text to a form using the label tool and you want a new line, then press **CONTROL+ENTER** (if you just press **ENTER** Access thinks you have finished entering text into the label).

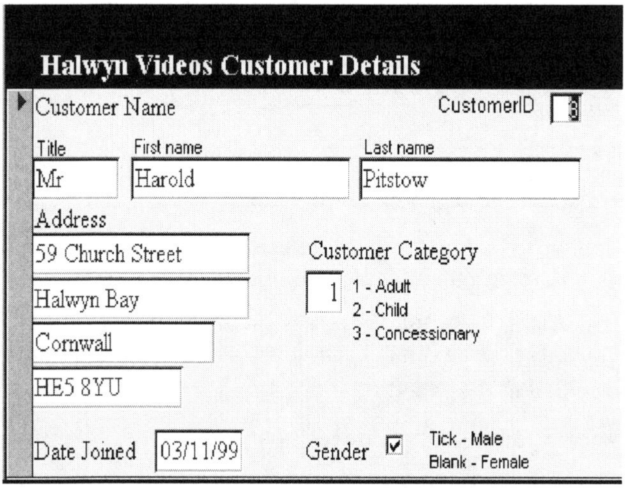

Halwyn Videos Customer Details

Customer Name   CustomerID

| Title | First name | Last name |
| Mr | Harold | Pitstow |

Address

59 Church Street

Customer Category

Halwyn Bay   1   1 - Adult
2 - Child

Cornwall   3 - Concessionary

HE5 8YU

Date Joined   03/11/99   Gender ☑   Tick - Male
Blank - Female

FIGURE 14.3

Portfolio items

VideoEntry form.

CustomerEntry form.

More on reports

Topic objectives

This topic explores some of the basic tools for designing your own reports rather than using the standard reports that can be created using AutoReport or ReportWizard. You will already have met a number of the tools which are used in report design, in Topic 14 when you were learning how to design forms. These tools will be used again in this topic, and you will have the opportunity to see how you can apply your learning in a different context.

This topic shows you how to:

- understand the components of a report
- create a blank report as a basis for later design work
- create a report to your own design
- add lines and rectangles to reports and forms.

Components of a report

The components of a report are listed and described below.

Component	Function
Report Header	Contains any headings or other introductory text which might appear at the beginning of the report.
Page Header	Contains headings that will appear at the top of each page, such as a running title and page numbers.
Detail	Shows data from the records in the database. Sets up the format for records in general, which is then used for every record to be included in the report.
Page Footer	Appears at the bottom of each page.
Report Footer	Contains information at the end of the report, such as a final summary or a statement such as 'this is the end of the report'.
Group Header	Marks the beginning of a group, usually introduces the group that the report will display.
Group Footer	Marks the end of a group and often contains sections which summarise the records that are part of a group.

Examine the report **CustomersRep** created with Report Wizard in Topic 12:

1 With the Database window displayed, click on **REPORTS**, select this report, and then click on **DESIGN**.

2 Note that Report Wizard creates reports with default settings in many areas of the report.

3 Examine the report that you have displayed.

4 Click on each control in turn. What are the default settings for:
(a) Report Header
(b) Page Header
(c) Group Header
(d) Detail
(e) Group Footer
(f) Page Footer
(g) Report Footer?

Creating a new blank report

There are two ways to create your own report: start with a new blank report, or create a 'quick and dirty' report using Report Wizard, and then modify that report. We used the second of these approaches in Topic 15 when we were creating new forms. Here we use the other approach, simply to extend your experience and skills. Both routes are equally acceptable and can be used for forms and reports.

To create a new report, without the aid of Report Wizard:

1 Choose **REPORTS** in the objects list of the Database window and click on the **NEW** button.

2 Click on the **DOWN ARROW** button of the **CHOOSE THE TABLE OR QUERY...** list box, to produce a list of tables and queries and select the table for which you wish to create a report. Choose the **CUSTOMER** table.

3 Select the **DESIGN VIEW** option to create a report without using Report Wizard. Click on **OK**.

4 Display the field list by choosing **VIEW-FIELD LIST**.

5 Add all the fields to the report from the field list. Display the field list and double-click on the **FIELD LIST** title bar to highlight all the fields.

6 Click and drag the highlighted fields onto the **Detail** section of the report. Controls for all the fields should appear.

7 Save as *Customer* and close. You will open this report later to modify its layout.

Customising a report

You are asked to improve on the design of the report **Customer**, which was created above, so that the final report looks as shown in Figure 15.1.

1 First open the existing report. Select the report **Customer** in the Database window and then click on the **DESIGN** button.

2 Move the controls on the report until it resembles the Design screen in Figure 15.1. If the toolbox is in the way, you can drag it out of the way or use **VIEW-TOOLBOX** to close it. If you get into a muddle, remember that controls can be

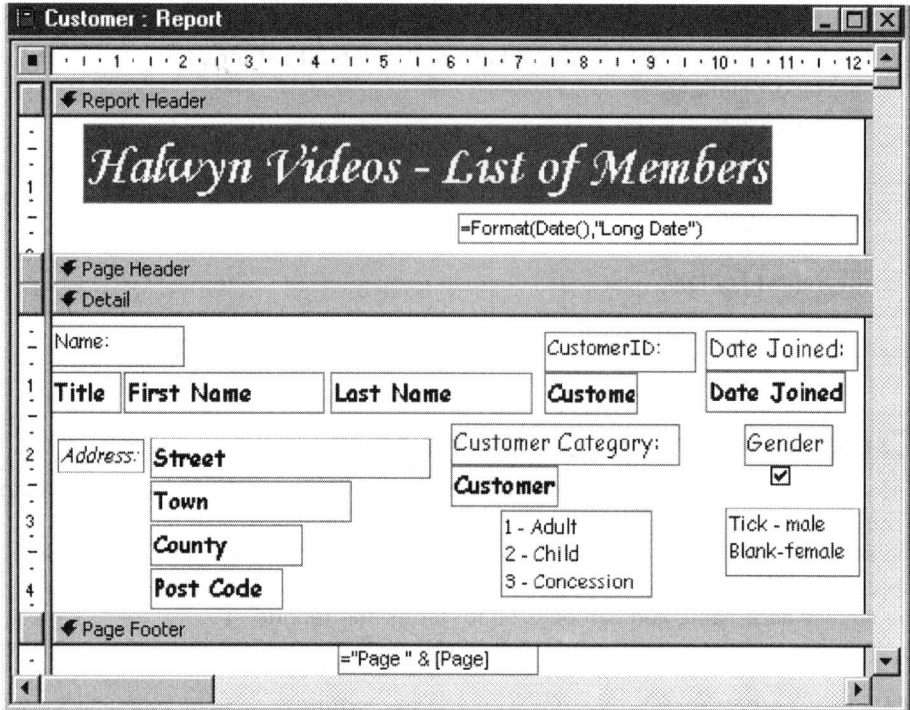

FIGURE 15.1

deleted by selecting them and using the **DELETE** key. If all else fails close *without saving* and start again.

3 View the new report on screen using **PRINT PREVIEW**.

4 Save the report as ***Customer***. Do not close the report.

5 Return to Design view. Take out the individual labels for the fields that belong to the address. Add a general label ***Address***, next to the appropriate fields. Do the same for the fields that relate to the name.

6 Create labels into which you can insert text, by displaying the toolbox and clicking on the **LABEL** tool. Click in the **Detail** section and add text to define **Customer Category** and **Gender**.

7 Press **ENTER** or click on another part of the report to complete changes.

8 Select and change the font and font size of any of the controls for which this might be appropriate.

9 Try aligning groups of controls to achieve a tidy-looking report, using **FORMAT-ALIGN-LEFT** to align a group of controls. (Select them as a group first.)

10 Next create a report header and a report footer by choosing **VIEW-REPORT HEADER/FOOTER** so that a tick is placed beside this option.

11 Create a label into which you can insert the heading text, by displaying the toolbox and clicking on the **LABEL** tool. Click in the **Report Header** band at the point where the text is to begin.

12 Type the text in the report header as shown in Figure 15.1.

⑬ Select the control in the report header, and choose a font, size and colour if you wish. If necessary, stretch the control box to display all of the text. You can centre align the text within the label by clicking on the **CENTER** button.

⑭ Choose **INSERT-PAGE NUMBERS** and select **PAGE N** format and choose the **BOTTOM OF PAGE (FOOTER)** option. Leave **ALIGNMENT** as **CENTER** and **SHOW NUMBER ON FIRST PAGE** ticked. Click on **OK**. Perform any font or other formatting that you might feel to be appropriate.

⑮ Adjust the depths of the sections, print preview the report, save the report as *Customer* and close the report.

Note: You may need to move back and forth between Print Preview and Design view a few times before you are satisfied with your design.

Halwyn Videos - List of Members

22 June 2001

FIGURE 15.2

Name:			CustomerID:	Date Joined:
Mr	Pete	Brown	1	15/10/98

Address: **18 Davy Close**   Customer Category: Gender
Halwyn Bay   **1**   ☑
Cornwall   1 - Adult   Tick - male
HE5 6TR   2 - Child   Blank-female
                                  3 - Concession

Adding lines and rectangles

Access offers a wide range of tools for formatting both screens and reports and supports the imaginative creation of interesting screens and reports. These include: lines and rectangles, dimensions, colours and borders. Here we briefly introduce the use of lines and rectangles. If you are interested in the other features please refer to the companion book, *Access 2000 An Advanced Course for Students*.

Lines and rectangles can be added to reports and forms to emphasis portions of the form or report or to separate one part of the form or report from another.

To add lines:

- Select the **LINE** tool in the toolbox.
- Point to where you want the line to start.
- Drag the pointer. The **LINE** tool draws a line from where you start dragging the pointer to where you release the mouse.

To add rectangles:

- Select the **RECTANGLE** tool in the toolbox.
- Point to where you want the corner of the rectangle to be.
- Drag the pointer to where you want the opposite corner to be.

Now add some lines and rectangles to your report **Customer:**

① Open the report in Design view.

② Add a rectangle around the heading in the report header band.

3 Add a line under the detail band, so that there is a line at the bottom of each record.

4 Add lines or rectangles in any other positions where you think that they might make the report more legible.

5 Find out how to change the weight of lines and rectangles, and adjust the lines accordingly.

6 Save the report as *Customer*.

Portfolio item

Customer report.

Relational databases

Topic objectives

Throughout this book, any queries, forms or reports we have created have been based on one table, either the **Video** table or the **Customer** table. A relational database management system, such as Access, allows more than one table to be created in a database and allows links between these tables, using common fields, to be established. This topic introduces the concept of a relational database.

This topic shows you how to:

- understand the concept of a relational database
- establish a small relational database by linking the **Video** and **Customer** tables through the creation of a **Video Loan** table.

Through fields, such as **VideoID**, which are common to both the **Video** and **Video Loan** tables, a link between the two tables can be established. Linking **Video Loan** to the Customer table through **CustomerID** enables the database to tell you which customers are borrowing which videos. This topic provides a brief introduction to the construction of a simple relational database.

To learn more about relational databases you should move on to *Access 2000 An Advanced Course for Students*.

Introducing relationships

We have created two tables, one that lists the video rental stock of Halwyn Videos, and another that lists details of their customers. We have demonstrated that some useful queries and reports can be created on the basis of these tables, but whilst we are working with tables alone, we cannot record transactions, such as the loan of a video to a specific customer. In order to do this we need to create a new table called **Video Loan** and to link this to the existing **Video** and **Customer** tables.

You may wonder why we couldn't just add some more fields to the **Customer** table to record what the customers have borrowed.

If we added fields to the **Customer** table, such as **Video Title** (or better still **VideoID**) and **Date Hired**, we could record when a customer hired a video. When they brought it back the data in these fields could be deleted (but we would have to be careful not to delete any other fields in the record). What if the customer wanted to borrow two, three or more videos? You could restrict them to one loan at once but then the customers might go elsewhere for better service. You could add more fields for each loan but this tends to get fiddly.

Although it may seem extra work to create a new table and then link it to the other tables, it is simpler in the long run to do this, as you are less likely to get in a mess with the data. People who design database systems usually prefer many smaller linked tables to fewer larger tables, as the data is more manageable in smaller sets. Each set of data (which is stored as a table) usually concerns a 'thing'. A loan is a 'thing', which is a loan – it is *not* a video or a customer, they are separate 'things'.

If we create a **Video Loan** table, and record **VideoID**, **CustomerID** and **Date Hired**, for instance, when the video is returned the record in the table can be deleted (and we don't have to worry about deleting some fields and not others). Better still, the record could be cut and pasted into an **Archive** table, which the business might find useful to discover which videos are borrowed most often and who the regular customers are.

Creating the *Video Loan* table

First let's review the fields in the existing two tables. Note that the fields **CustomerID** and **VideoID**, come into their own as unique identifiers of specific records. You might be tempted to use another field, such as the **Title** field, to identify a record in the Video table. Titles of videos are, however, not unique. Quite apart from remakes of old classics under the same title, two copies of the same film might be in stock, one being on DVD and the other VHS. Similarly, the only unique field in the **Customer** table is the **CustomerID**.

Video Table	**Customer Table**
VideoID	CustomerID
Title	First Name
Video Category	Last Name
Censor Rating	Title
Date of Acquisition	Street
Format	Town
Cost	County
	Post Code
	Telephone No
	Member Type
	Date of Joining

Now let's think about how we might link these two tables together. Customers and videos are linked by the transaction of a loan. If we create the **Video Loan** table, with the fields indicated below, we can use this to keep a record of loans. Note that by using the fields **CustomerID** and **VideoID** in the table **Video Loan**, we have created a common field between the **Customers** and **Videos** table, and the **Video Loan** table, respectively.

The simplest **Video Loan** table would contain the following fields:

Loan No	AutoNumber
Date Hired	Date/time
VideoID	Number – long integer
CustomerID	Number – long integer

1 In the Database window, click on the **TABLES** object. Click on the **NEW** button.

2 Choose Design view and set up the fields as shown in the table above.

3 Set the **Loan No** field as the primary key. Save the table as *Video Loan*.

	Field Name	Data Type	
🔑	Loan No	AutoNumber	
	CustomerID	Number	Long Integer
	VideoID	Number	Long Integer
	Date Hired	Date/Time	

4 Using **TOOLS-ANALYZE-DOCUMENTOR**, print the properties of the **Video Loan** table.

Linking the *Video Loan* table to the *Video* and *Customer* tables

1 Close the **Video Loan** table. Make sure that all tables, forms and reports are closed so that just the Database Window is left open.

Now the relationship between **Video ID** in the **Video** table and **VideoID** in the **Video Loan** table can be created. The data type of the field **VideoID** (in **Video Loan**) is a long integer number, which is compatible with the data type AutoNumber of the field **VideoID** (in **Video**). Choose **TOOLS-RELATIONSHIPS** and the **RELATIONSHIPS** dialog box appears with the **SHOW TABLE** dialog box within it. (If the **SHOW TABLE** dialog box does not appear, click on the **SHOW TABLE** button on the toolbar.)

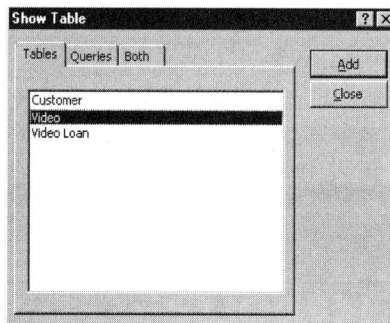

FIGURE 16.1

2 Select **Video** and click on **ADD**. Select **Video Loan** and click on **ADD**. Click on **CLOSE**. The two table windows should be displayed and you may re-size them if you wish.

3 To create the relationship, click on the **VideoID** field in the **Video** table and drag to the **VideoID** field in the **Video Loan** table. **IMPORTANT**: drag *from* **Video** table *to* **Video Loan** table. Release and the **EDIT RELATIONSHIPS** dialog box is displayed.

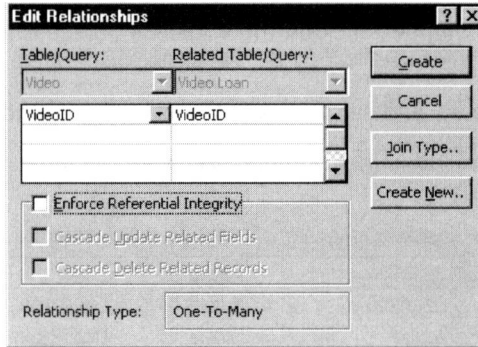

FIGURE 16.2

4 Click on **CREATE** and the relationship between the tables will be shown.

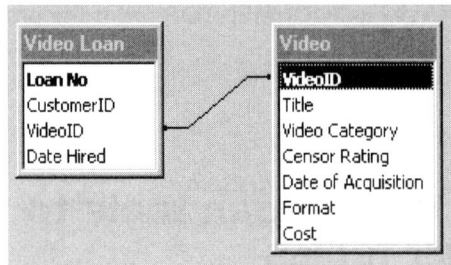

FIGURE 16.3

5 Use **FILE-SAVE** to save changes to the layout.

6 Click on the **SHOW TABLE** button on the toolbar. Select **Customer** and click on **ADD**. Click on **CLOSE**. There should now be three table windows displayed.

7 To create the relationship, click on the **CustomerID** field in the **Customer** table and drag to the **CustomerID** field in the **Video Loan** table. **IMPORTANT**: drag *from* **Customer** table *to* **Video Loan** table. Release and the **EDIT RELATIONSHIPS** dialog box will be displayed.

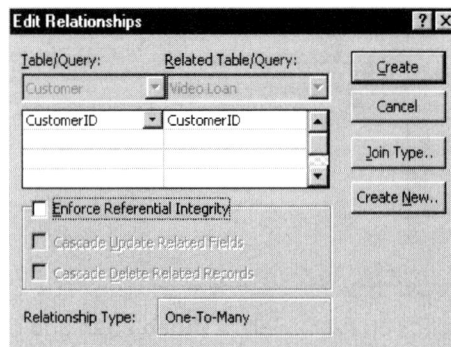

FIGURE 16.4

8 Click on **OK** and the relationship between the tables will be shown. Use **FILE-SAVE** to save changes to the layout.

9 To print the relationships choose **FILE-PRINT RELATIONSHIPS** and a preview will be displayed. Click on the **PRINT** button. Close the Relationships report without saving, and save and close the Relationships window.

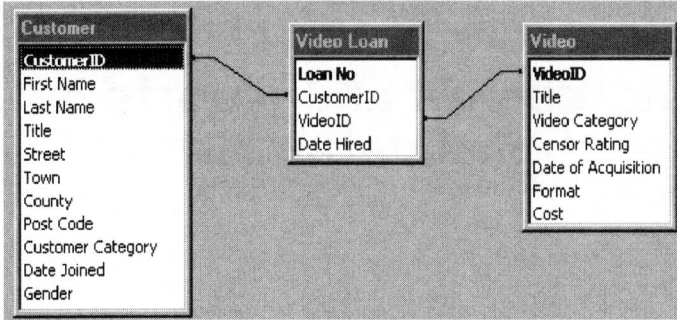

FIGURE 16.5

In the next topic we shall design a form for entering some data into the **Video Loan** table.

Portfolio items

Video Loan table.

Relationships between **Video**, **Video Loan** and **Customer** tables.

Forms, queries and reports in relational databases

Topic objectives

By defining a relationship between two or more tables, the tables can appear to act as one table, and you can generate forms, queries and reports from them. With the links between the tables established, this topic shows you how to:

- create a form that uses drop-down lists based on the **Video** and **Customer** tables for entering data into the **Video Loan** table
- investigate the way Access displays datasheet data of linked tables
- create queries and reports using the three tables in the database.

Creating the *Video Loan* form

1 Use **AUTOFORM – TABULAR** to create a form based on the **Video Loan** table. It should look similar to the one below.

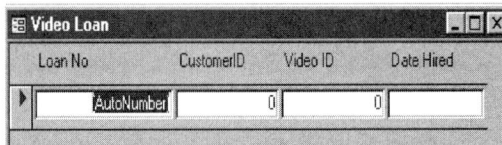

FIGURE 17.1

🖼 Video Loan			_ □ ×
Loan No	CustomerID	Video ID	Date Hired
▶	AutoNumber	0	0	

2 View the form in Design view and delete the **CustomerID** control. Widen the **Detail** section by dragging the lower separator down.

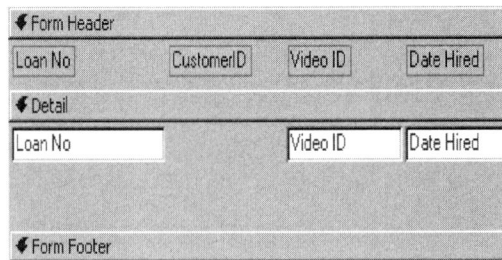

FIGURE 17.2

> ✦ Form Header
>
> | Loan No | | CustomerID | Video ID | | Date Hired |
>
> ✦ Detail
>
> | Loan No | | | Video ID | Date Hired |
>
> ✦ Form Footer

3 Check that the toolbox is displayed (it may be vertically at the side of the screen or horizontally at the top or bottom), if not use **VIEW-TOOLBOX** to display it. Ensure that the Wizard button is depressed (it is top of second column in the illustration) and click on the **COMBO BOX** button. Now click in the middle of the space you have created in the detail section.

4 The Combo Box Wizard starts, select **I WANT THE COMBO BOX TO LOOK UP VALUES IN A TABLE OR QUERY** and click on **NEXT>**.

5 Select the **Customer** table and click on **NEXT>**. Add the fields **CustomerID**, **Last Name** and **First Name** in this order and click on **NEXT>**.

The next box displays the customer list, click **NEXT>** again.

6 Choose the option **STORE THAT VALUE IN THIS FIELD** and select **CustomerID** from the list. Click **NEXT>** and **FINISH**.

7 You should see a drop-down style control in the detail section. As there is a label in the Form Header section select the label (click on it) and delete it.

FIGURE 17.3

8 Drag the **VideoID** and **Date Hired** controls and their labels to the right to make a larger gap into which you can drag the new **CustomerID** control.

9 Now delete the **VideoID** control and repeat the steps above, this time selecting the Video table, choosing the fields **VideoID** and **Title** and storing the value in **VideoID**.

10 Delete the label that appears with the new control and rearrange the controls so that they are all in line again. Edit the labels in the Form header to read **Customer and Video**. Finally make the detail section narrower and save the form as **Video Loan**.

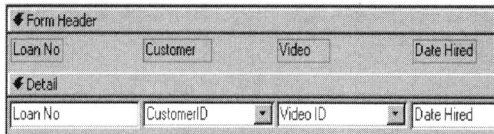

FIGURE 17.4

89

11 Run the form and use it to enter about ten records.

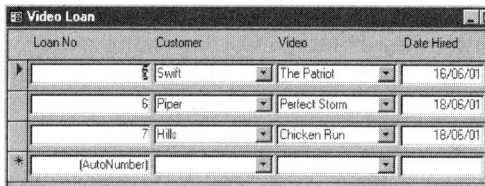

FIGURE 17.5

Datasheets in relational databases

Through the datasheet it is now possible to see loan records that belong to particular customers.

1 Open the **Customer** table in Datasheet view. Notice that there is an additional column of plus symbols. Click on one these plus symbols and **Insert Subdata sheet** appears.

2 Select **Video Loan** and the link field **CustomerID** will be automatically selected. Click on **OK**.

3 The subdatasheet for the selected record should appear. If that customer has borrowed any videos they will be listed in the subdatasheet. Notice that the plus symbol becomes a minus and clicking on the minus symbol hides the subdatasheet.

FIGURE 17.6

Subdatasheets can be displayed for any customers. Data can be entered or amended through the subdatasheet. If you wish to remove the subdatasheet altogether use **FORMAT-SUBDATASHEET-REMOVE**.

Creating queries and reports based on linked tables

This task will use the **Video Loan** table, and the **Customer** and **Video** tables to create a list of videos borrowed.

1 Create a new query in Design view and, in turn, add each of the three tables. The tables should be linked.

2 Add the fields **Title**, **First Name**, and **Last Name** from the **Customer** table; **Title**, from the **Video** table, and **Date Hired** from the **Video Loan** table. Sort the **Date Hired** in descending order. View the query and save it as *Videos On Loan*.

3 Create a report based on this query. Save the report as *Videos On Loan*.

It might be useful to see how many videos each borrower has on loan.

1 Open the **Video Loan** form and add some more records so that some customers have borrowed more than one video.

2 Create a new query and add the **Customer** and **Video Loan** tables. Add the fields **Last Name** and **First Name** from the **Customer** table and **Loan No** from the **Video Loan** table.

3 Click on the **TOTALS** button and set **LOAN NO** to **COUNT**. Save the query as *Multiple Rentals*.

4 Design, save and print a report *Multiple Rentals* based on this query.

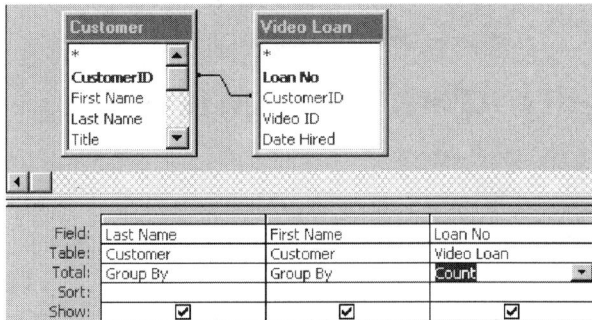

FIGURE 17.7

Having made the database relational by linking the tables we have increased the flexibility with which we can work with the data. However, there is still room for improvement, which leads us to the next topic.

Portfolio items

Video Loan table.

Videos On Loan (query and report).

Multiple Rentals (query and report).

Making improvements

Topic objectives

As you work with a database application such as this one for a video rental business you begin to see other ways in which it could provide useful information, for example returns that are overdue. Even experienced database designers need to make modifications as they develop applications, and for small changes this is relatively straightforward. This topic shows you how to:

▨ add a **Date Returned** field to the **Video Loan** table
▨ add a rental rate.

Adding a field to a table

In an ideal situation, all the fields needed for a database application would be set up when a table is first created. However, the need for some data may not be perceived at the initial stages of creating the database. An example might be to add a field called **Initials** to the **Customer** database so that these could appear on address labels instead of the first name.

A deliberate omission in the **Video Loan** table has been made. We know when a video was borrowed but we do not know when (or if) it has been returned. A **Date Returned** field will allow any overdue loans to be identified.

1 Select **TABLES** in the **OBJECTS** column of the Database window, highlight the **Video Loan** table and click on the **DESIGN** button.

2 In the next row, add the **Date Returned** field and select its data type as **DATE/ TIME**. Under **FORMAT OF THE PROPERTIES** select **SHORT DATE**.

3 Save the changes and close the table. If you view the datasheet you will see that there is an extra column for the new field but there is no data.

4 Data can be added directly into the datasheet or, as this data is in 'code' (using **CustomerID** and **VideoID**, it would be better to use the **Video Loan** form.

5 Close the datasheet and click on the **FORMS** object and open the **Video Loan** form. There is no **Date Returned** field because the table was modified after the form was designed.

6 The form requires some simple modification, so click on the **DESIGN VIEW** button to display the form in design view. Identify the field list which should look like the illustration. If the list is not visible, click on the **FIELD LIST** button.

(7) Widen the detail section and drag the **Date Returned** field from the **Video Loan** field list and drop it in the space you have just made in the detail section.

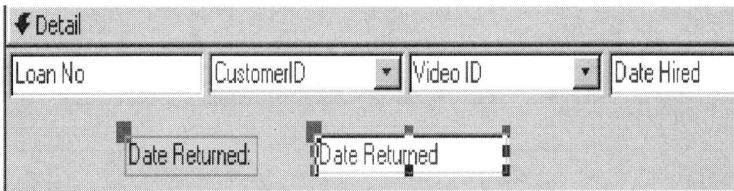

FIGURE 18.1

(8) Widen the form design window and drag the edge of the form to the right. Select the label of the **Date Returned** control and use **EDIT-CUT**. Click on the **Form Header** bar and used **EDIT-PASTE**. The label will be pasted into the top left corner of the header section. Drag the label to the right to make the next header in the row. Drag the **Date Returned** control in line with the other controls and return the size of the detail section to its original depth.

(9) Run the form and use it to enter some return dates. Design a query and a report based on that query to select those records where there isn't a date entered in the **Date Returned** field. *Hint:* use the criteria **Null** in the query grid. Null means there is no entry in the field. Save your query and report as *Overdue Videos*.

FIGURE 18.2

Adding a rental rate

The only cost dealt with so far is the price originally paid for the video. If all the videos cost the same to rent per day then all that would be needed would be to work out the number of days the video was hired for and to multiply that by the daily charge, say, £2.

(1) Create a query based on the **Video Loan** table and add the fields **Date Hired** and **Date Returned**. In the criteria row of the **Date Returned** field, put the criterion *Is Not Null* to select videos that have been returned. Should you also put *Is Not Null* in the **Date Hired** field? This data should not be missing but if it is then *Is Not Null* will prevent these records from being selected. The foolproof way to ensure data is entered into the **Date Hired** field is to set its **Required property** to **Yes**. To do this, first check that there is data for **Date Hired** in every record, then view the **Video Loan** table in Design view and set the **Required property** to **Yes**.

(2) Run the query and you should see only records where there is data in both fields. These two fields can be used to work out the number of days the video has been out on loan and consequently the amount paid for the rental. Return to the query design to add calculated fields to the query.

③ Set up the query grid as illustrated below. It is important to get the punctuation right. The two headings are *Days hired: [Date Returned]-[Date Hired]* and *Rental: [Days Hired]*2*.

④ Right-click on the **Rental** column and set the **Format property** to **currency**.

FIGURE 18.3

Field:	Date Hired	Date Returned	Days hired: [Date Returned]-[Date Hired]	Rental: [Days Hired]*2
Table:	Video Loan	Video Loan		
Sort:				
Show:	☑	☑	☑	☑
Criteria:		Is Not Null		

⑤ Save the query as *Rental fees* and run it. Use the Report Wizard to create a Tabular report based on the **Rental fees** query. A calculated control can be added to the report footer. To add this control view the report in Design view.

⑥ Click on the **TEXT BOX** button `ab|` in the toolbox and click under **REPORT FOOTER** to drop a blank or 'unbound' control. Into the control text box, key in *=Sum([Rental])* – see illustration below. In the **Properties** 🗗 for this new control, set its **Name property** to **Rental Total** and its **Format property** to **Currency**. Save and preview.

94

FIGURE 18.4

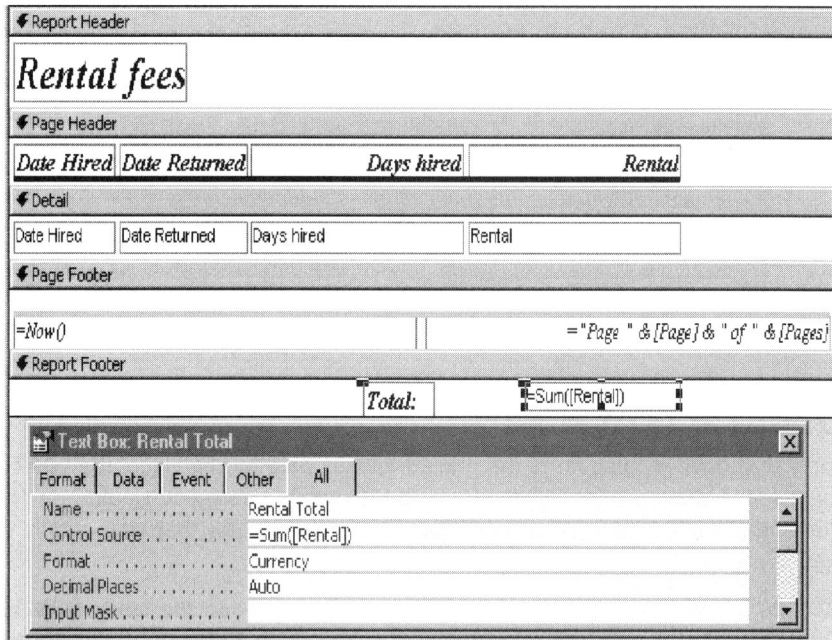

Adding a variety of rental rates

This section takes the modifications further and is a little more complex, so you may omit it if you wish.

In order to set a different rental rate for each video, an extra field could be added to the **Video** table which held the daily rental rate. Consider what would happen if the rate for latest releases was to increase from £2 to £2.25. This would mean updating all the latest release records in the **Video** table. Even if you used **FIND AND REPLACE** you might miss some, so the best way is to create a table of rental fees. A number of fee categories can be identified and each video can be allocated a category.

If you add a **Rental Category** field to the **Video** table, this can be linked to the **Rental fees** table so that the daily charge can be ascertained. If the charges are revised then only the list of fees in the **Rental fees** table need be altered.

1 Create a **Rental fees** table by choosing the **TABLES** object in the Database Window, clicking on **NEW** and choosing **DESIGN VIEW**.

2 Set up three fields as shown in the illustration. Note that the **Required** property for **Rental fees** is set to **Yes**, meaning that this field cannot be left blank.

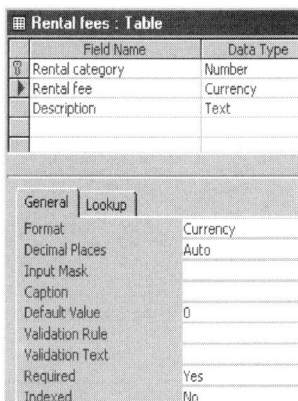

FIGURE 18.5

3 Switch to Datasheet view and add the following data

Rental category	Rental fees	Description
1	£2.00	Latest release
2	£1.50	Normal
3	£1.00	Childrens/Special offer

FIGURE 18.6

4 Close the table. Open the **Video** table in Design view and add a **Rental Category** field. Accept the default properties for this field.

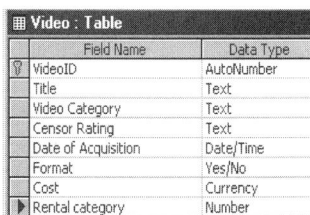

FIGURE 18.7

5 Switch to Datasheet view and fill in a rental category for each record. You could consider setting a validation rule for this field (try **<4** and set an appropriate message in the **Validation Text property**). Close the table.

6 Open the **Relationships** window using **TOOLS-RELATIONSHIPS**, click on the **ADD TABLE** button and add the **Rental fees** table.

7 Drag the **Rental Category** field *from* the **Rental fees** table *to* the **Rental category** field in the **Video** table and click on **CREATE** to set up the relationship. Save and close the **Relationships** window.

8 Click on QUERIES in the object list and click on NEW and DESIGN VIEW. Add the tables **Rental fees**, **Video** and **Video Loan** to the query. Drag on the fields **Date Hired** and **Date Returned** from the **Video Loan** table, and **Rental fees** from the **Rental fees** table. Note that we are not including any fields from the **Video** table but that this table is the link between the other two tables.

9 Create two calculated fields as shown. Save the query as *Rental fees2* and run it.

FIGURE 18.8

Field:	Days hired: [Date Returned]-[Date Hired]		Rental: [Days Hired]*[Rental fee]	
Table:				
Sort:				
Show:		☑		☑
Criteria:				

10 Close the query. In the same manner as you created a report for **Rental fees**, create the report *Rental fees2* based on the **Rental fees2** query.

Note: Having added a field to the **Video** table means that you will need to modify any forms or reports created from the **Video** table if you want the new field to appear on them.

Portfolio items

Modified **Video Loan** form.

Overdue Videos (query and report).

Rental Fees (query and report).

Rental Fees2 (query and report).

Switchboard forms

Topic objectives

A database application is designed to give easy access to forms and reports through an easy-to-use interface. A **switchboard** form provides this database application interface. It is a special form that allows you to open forms and reports that you have created, from a central menu.

The switchboard form has buttons that you can click to allow you to perform various tasks. For example, a form can be opened to allow the entry of a new record, or a monthly report (e.g. new customers) can be printed at the click of a button in the switchboard form.

A switchboard form can have more than one 'page', but in this topic we shall only create a single-page switchboard form. The companion book *Access 2000 An Advanced Course for Students* deals with switchboard forms with more than one page.

This topic will show you how to:

- create a switchboard form
- set the switchboard form to automatically open when the database is opened
- edit a switchboard form.

97

Creating a switchboard form

To create a switchboard form by using the Switchboard Manager:

1 Choose **TOOLS-DATABASE UTILITIES**, and select **SWITCHBOARD MANAGER**.

2 If you have not created a switchboard then Access will ask you if you would like to create a switchboard, choose **YES**.

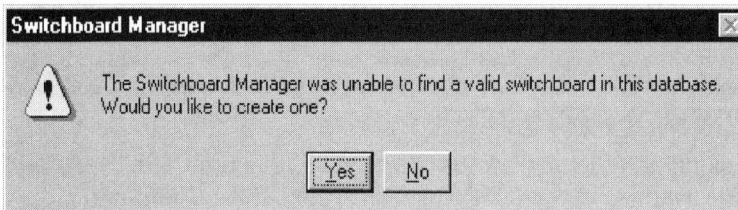

Switchboard Manager

The Switchboard Manager was unable to find a valid switchboard in this database. Would you like to create one?

Yes   No

FIGURE 19.1

3 In the **SWITCHBOARD MANAGER** dialog box, click on the **EDIT** button. In the **EDIT SWITCHBOARD PAGE** dialog box, type the name, *Main Menu*, for the switchboard in the **SWITCHBOARD NAME** box, and then click **NEW**.

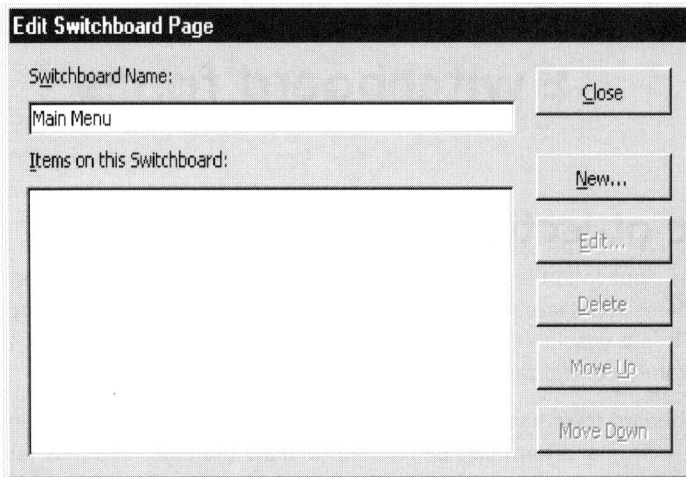

FIGURE 19.2

```
Edit Switchboard Page

Switchboard Name:                              [  Close  ]
[Main Menu                              ]

Items on this Switchboard:                     [  New...  ]

┌─────────────────────────────────┐           [  Edit...  ]
│                                 │
│                                 │           [  Delete  ]
│                                 │
│                                 │           [  Move Up  ]
│                                 │
│                                 │           [ Move Down ]
└─────────────────────────────────┘
```

④ In the **EDIT SWITCHBOARD ITEM** dialog box, type the text, *Add New Video*, for the first switchboard button in the **TEXT** box. Open the **COMMAND** box and select **OPEN FORM IN ADD MODE**, and in the **Form** box select the form **Video**. Click on **OK**.

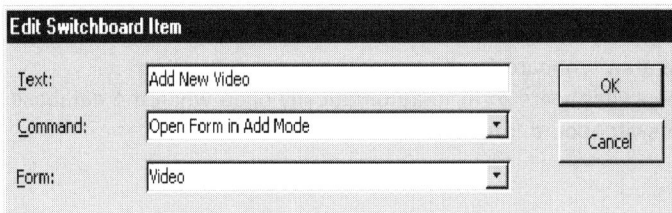

FIGURE 19.3

```
Edit Switchboard Item

Text:     [Add New Video                  ]        [   OK   ]

Command:  [Open Form in Add Mode        ▼]        [ Cancel ]

Form:     [Video                         ▼]
```

⑤ Steps 3 and 4 are repeated for all further items to be added to the switchboard. Click on **NEW** to add another menu item, this time **TEXT** – *Amend Video details*, **COMMAND** (select from drop-down list) – **OPEN FORM IN EDIT MODE**, **FORM** (select from drop-down list) – **Video**.

⑥ Click on **NEW** to add another menu item, this time **TEXT** – *Add New Customer*, **COMMAND** – **OPEN FORM IN ADD MODE**, **FORM** – **Customer**.

⑦ Click on **NEW** to add another menu item, this time **TEXT** – *Amend Customer details*, **COMMAND** – **OPEN FORM IN EDIT MODE**, **FORM** – **Customer**.

⑧ Click on **NEW** to add another menu item, this time **TEXT** – *Print Video list*, **COMMAND** – **OPEN REPORT**, **REPORT** – **Video**.

⑨ Click on **NEW** to add another menu item, this time **TEXT** – *Print Customer list*, **COMMAND** – **OPEN REPORT**, **REPORT** – **Customer**.

⑩ Close the Switchboard Manager by clicking on the **CLOSE** button.

⑪ Click the **FORMS** object and open the **Switchboard** form. Click each button in turn to test that buttons function as expected. If they don't you may need to edit the form (see Editing the switchboard form).

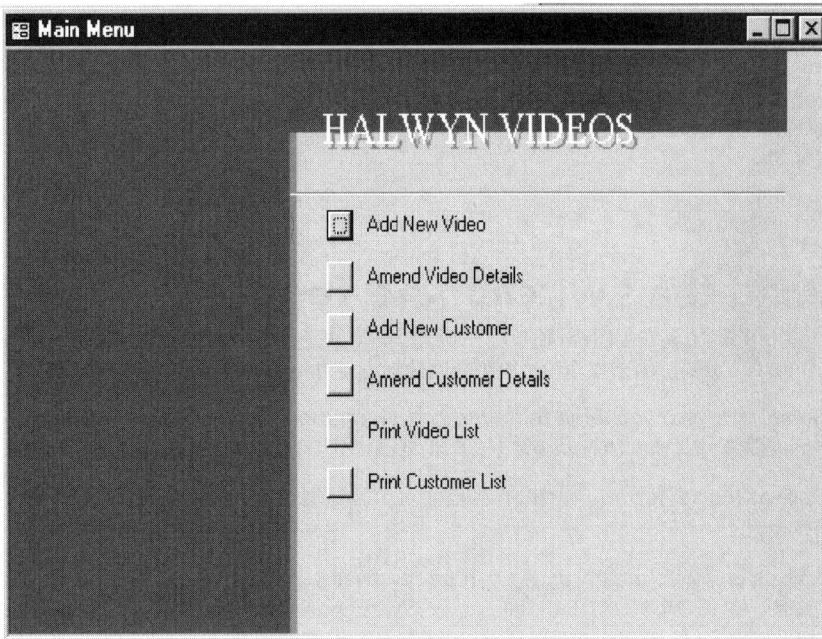

FIGURE 19.4

If you want to edit or delete an item, click the item in the **ITEMS ON THIS SWITCHBOARD** box, and then click **EDIT** or **DELETE**. If you want to rearrange items, click the item in the box, and then click **MOVE UP** or **MOVE DOWN**.

IMPORTANT: when you create a switchboard with the Switchboard Manager, Access creates a **Switchboard Items** table that describes what the buttons on the form display. Don't make any changes to this table as you may stop the switchboard form from working properly.

99

Display the switchboard form when the database opens

The following setting will make the switchboard form open automatically as soon as the database opens.

1 Choose **TOOLS-STARTUP**.

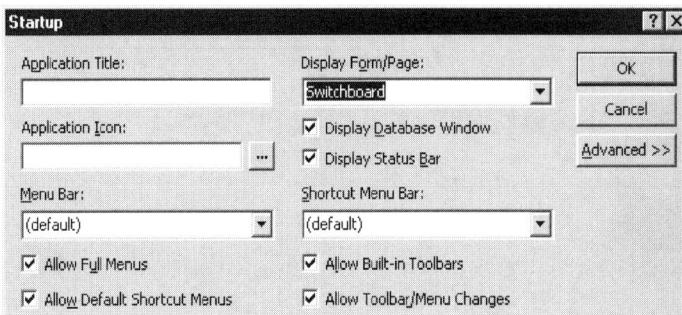

FIGURE 19.5

2 Open the **DISPLAY FORM/PAGE** drop-down list box, and choose **SWITCHBOARD**. Click on **OK**.

Note: Changes to these settings in the **STARTUP** dialog box will not take effect until the next time the database is opened. If you want to stop the Switchboard form opening automatically then set **DISPLAY FORM/PAGE** back to **(NONE)** in the **STARTUP** dialog box.

Editing the switchboard form

1. Using **TOOLS-DATABASE UTILITIES,** open the Switchboard Manager, choose **MAIN MENU** from the switchboard pages list and click on **EDIT**.

2. Select the item you wish to edit and click on the **EDIT** button. Make changes to the **TEXT, COMMAND** and **FORM/REPORT** boxes as required. Click **OK**.

3. Repeat step 2 for any further editing operations as required. Close the Switchboard Manager.

Note: Items on switchboard pages can be removed using the **DELETE** button in the **EDIT SWITCHBOARD PAGE** dialog box. Switchboard pages can be removed using the **DELETE** button in the **SWITCHBOARD MANAGER** dialog box.

Portfolio item

Switchboard form.

APPENDIX I – Data

Video table

It is not necessary to key all these titles into the **Video** table. You can start with about 20 records and selectively add records for queries in the book. Alternatively you can download a spreadsheet of this data from the website www.learningmatters.co.uk and import it into your table. The data for the **VideoID** field is deliberately omitted as Access will number the records. The actual **VideoID** number for each record is not important and you can enter the records below in any order you wish. For the Format field, tick those records with a VHS format and leave blank those with DVD format.

Title	Video Category	Censor Rating	Date of Acquisition	Format	Cost
Deep Blue Sea	Drama	18	30/12/99	VHS	£5.00
Buffy Series III	Sci Fi	15	13/06/00	DVD	£5.25
Gladiator	Action	15	13/06/00	VHS	£6.75
The Beach	Drama	15	23/06/00	DVD	£6.75
The Patriot	Action	15	24/06/00	VHS	£6.75
Big Momma's House	Comedy	12	24/06/00	VHS	£10.00
Perfect Storm	Drama	12	24/06/00	VHS	£5.00
Mission: Impossible 2	Action	15	24/06/00	VHS	£5.00
Stir of Echoes	Thriller	15	16/08/00	VHS	£7.00
Maybe Baby	Comedy	15	16/08/00	VHS	£7.00
Final Destination	Horror	15	17/09/00	VHS	£7.50
Frequency	Drama	15	19/10/00	VHS	£6.75
Essex Boys	Thriller	18	19/10/00	VHS	£5.25
Whole Nine Yards	Comedy	15	19/10/00	DVD	£5.25
Chicken Run	Childrens	U	21/10/00	VHS	£5.00
Kevin & Perry Go Large	Comedy	15	24/01/01	VHS	£10.00
Erin Brockovich	Drama	15	24/01/01	VHS	£7.00
The Green Mile	Thriller	18	24/01/01	VHS	£10.00
28 Days	Drama	15	25/02/01	VHS	£7.00
Three to Tango	Comedy	12	20/03/01	VHS	£7.00
Toy Story 2	Childrens	U	20/03/01	VHS	£6.75
Jurassic Park	Childrens	PG	15/03/01	DVD	£6.75
Titanic	Drama	12	15/03/01	DVD	£5.25
Nutty Professor 2	Comedy	12	16/04/01	DVD	£10.00
Men in Black	Sci Fi	PG	31/05/01	VHS	£10.00
Star Trek Insurrection	Sci Fi	15	18/05/01	VHS	£10.00
Independence Day	Sci Fi	15	19/06/01	VHS	£5.00
The Full Monty	Comedy	15	19/06/01	DVD	£6.75
Doug's 1st Movie	Childrens	U	19/06/01	DVD	£8.00
End of Days	Action	18	21/07/01	VHS	£5.00
The Blair Witch Project	Horror	15	21/07/01	VHS	£5.00
The Mob Squad	Action	15	22/08/01	VHS	£8.00
The Out-of-towners	Comedy	12	22/08/01	VHS	£7.50

Title	Video Category	Censor Rating	Date of Acquisition	Format	Cost
Bringing out the Dead	Drama	18	29/09/01	VHS	£7.00
The Thirteenth Floor	Sci Fi	15	29/09/01	VHS	£6.75
Stigmata	Horror	18	29/09/01	DVD	£5.25
Limbo	Drama	15	29/09/01	DVD	£10.00
Molly	Drama	15	29/09/01	DVD	£10.00
Inspector Gadget	Comedy	U	15/10/01	DVD	£8.00
Angela's Ashes	Drama	15	15/10/01	DVD	£7.50
The Bone Collector	Thriller	15	15/10/01	DVD	£6.75
The Iron Giant	Childrens	U	15/10/01	VHS	£7.50
The World is not Enough	Thriller	12	17/11/01	VHS	£6.75
The Rage: Carrie 2	Horror	15	17/11/01	VHS	£10.00
Blue Streak	Comedy	12	17/11/01	DVD	£8.00
Runaway Bride	Comedy	PG	17/11/01	DVD	£7.50
K-911	Comedy	12	17/11/01	VHS	£7.50
The Sixth Sense	Thriller	15	18/12/01	VHS	£5.25
Austin Powers 2	Comedy	2	18/12/01	VHS	£8.00
Cube	Sci Fi	18	18/12/01	VHS	£8.50
The Matrix	Sci Fi	15	18/12/01	VHS	£5.25
Species 2	Sci Fi	18	18/12/01	DVD	£9.50
12 Monkeys	Sci Fi	15	18/12/01	VHS	£10.00
Notting Hill	Drama	15	15/01/02	VHS	£7.50
Python	Thriller	12	15/01/02	VHS	£5.50
Talos the Mummy	Horror	15	18/02/02	DVD	£8.50
Fast Getaway	Thriller	15	18/02/02	DVD	£12.00
Scream 2	Horror	15	18/02/02	VHS	£13.00
Wing Commander	Sci Fi	PG	18/02/02	VHS	£11.50
Rogue Trader	Drama	15	18/02/02	DVD	£8.50
Night Watch	Thriller	18	18/02/02	DVD	£7.50
Ronin	Thriller	15	18/02/02	DVD	£7.50
Outland	Sci Fi	15	18/02/02	DVD	£9.00
Knight in Camelot	Childrens	U	18/02/02	DVD	£8.50
The Patriot	Action	15	24/06/00	DVD	£8.00

Customer table

The data below is fairly sketchy and you will need to compose most of the data yourself. The fields below are only a guide and if you have additional fields such as **Gender** and **Customer Category** then you will need to compose data for these fields as well. **CustomerID** is deliberately left blank as Access will fill in this number provided you have set the data type to **AutoNumber**.

Customer ID	First Name	Last Name	Title	Street	Town	County	Post Code	Date Joined
	Pete	Brown	Mr	18 Davy Close	Halwyn Bay	Cornwall	HE5 6TR	15/10/98
	Lionel	Moroney	Mr	20 Baywater Rd	Withney	Cornwall	HE9 2EV	07/07/99
	Harry	Pitstow	Mr	7 Ship Street	Halwyn Bay	Cornwall	HE7 8YU	01/02/00
	Frances	Darcy	Miss	The Poplars	Halwyn Bay	Cornwall	HE6 4DU	12/12/99
	Aileen	Batley	Mrs	39 Ashford Drive	Halwyn Bay	Cornwall	HE6 7FN	07/03/00
	Ivor	Protheroe	Mr	16 Lowton Lane	Withney	Cornwall	ST10 2DZ	
	Freda	Swift	Miss	55 Cove Road	Halwyn Bay	Cornwall	HE3 8PS	
	Clifford	Hancock	Mr	47 High Street	Halwyn Bay	Cornwall	HE1 7JH	
	Robert	Banks	Mr	7 Horncroft Lane	Halwyn Bay	Cornwall	HE6 3DR	
	Freda	Badrock	Ms	6 High Street	Halwyn Bay	Cornwall	HE1 8YV	
	April	Maynard	Mrs	13 Withney Road	Halwyn Bay	Cornwall	HE4 5KD	
	June	Williams	Miss	8 Highwater Street	Halwyn Bay	Cornwall	HE10 4RT	
	Eileen	Drew	Mrs		Halwyn Bay	Cornwall		
	Beverley	Schofield	Miss		Halwyn Bay	Cornwall		
	Claire	Laycock	Ms		Halwyn Bay	Cornwall		
	Linda	Ashleigh	Mrs			Cornwall		
	Dinah	Turner	Miss			Cornwall		
	Leonard	Jones	Mr			Cornwall		
	Dick	Taylor	Mr			Cornwall		
	Fred	Barrett	Mr			Cornwall		
	Penelope	Pepper	Miss			Cornwall		
	Louis	Kent	Mr			Cornwall		
	Joseph	King	Mr			Cornwall		
	William	Farnham	Mr			Cornwall		
	Martyn	Rox	Ms			Cornwall		
	Sheila	Brown	Miss			Cornwall		
	Arthur	Davies	Mr			Cornwall		
	Edward	Bolden	Mr			Cornwall		

Topic 3

Halwyn Videos – **Video** table with 7 fields and 2 records ☐

Topic 4

Customer table ☐

Printout of the **Customer** table definition ☐

Printout of **Video** table definition ☐

Topic 5

Video table with lookup list for **Video Category** and data entered ☐

Customer table – with data entered ☐

Topic 6

Archived Customer table ☐

Topic 7

Printout of all **Video** table records ☐

Printout of all **Video** records sorted in **Category** order ☐

Printout of **Video** records filtered by **Category** and **Censor Rating** ☐

Printout of **Customer** table in Last Name order ☐

Printout of **Customer** table in Date of Joining order ☐

Printout of filtered **Customer** table ☐

Topic 8

Stock Check List (electronic and printout) ☐

Stock Currency query ☐

CustomersTelephone query ☐

CustomersJoin query ☐

CustomersAddress query ☐

Topic 9

Horror query based on **Video** table ☐

DVD query based on **Video** table ☐

Censor18 query based on **Video** table ☐

Old Vids query based on **Video** table ☐

Jurassic query based on **Video** table ☐

New Members query based on **Customer** table ☐

Topic 10

Queries: **Purchases May 01, Cost £5-£10, 12-15 Rating, Blue, Action and 15, Action or 15, Not PG, U** ☐

Sort1, Sort2 queries ☐

Category Count query ☐

Censor Rating Count query ☐

Category Totals query ☐

Topic 11

VideoCol screen form (created using AutoForm) ☐

VideoTab screen form (created using Form Wizard) ☐

CustomersCol screen form ☐

CustomersJus screen form ☐

Topic 12

VideoColR, a column report for the **Video** table ☐

Videos Listed by Date of Acquisition, a Tabular report for the **Video** table ☐

CustomersRep, a report for the **Customer** table ☐

Topic 13

Loyal Customers query ☐

Labels Loyal Customers report ☐

Loyal Customers mail merge letter ☐

Topic 14

VideoEntry form ☐

CustomerEntry form ☐

Topic 15

Customer report ☐

Topic 16

Video Loan table ☐

Relationships between **Video**, **Video Loan** and **Customer** tables ☐

Topic 17

Video Loan table ☐

Videos On Loan (query and report) ☐

Multiple Rentals (query and report) ☐

Topic 18

Modified **Video Loan** form ☐

Overdue Videos (query and report) ☐

Rental fees (query and report) ☐

Rental fees2 (query and report) ☐

Topic 19
Switchboard form

☐

Index

Access control menu, 6
Access database, 2
Access main menu, 6
Access window, 6
Alignment, controls, 75
AutoForm, 55
AutoReport, 61

Calculated fields, 93–94
Check boxes, 54
Closing
    database, 2
    form, 56
    report, 62
Close button, 6
Colours, 73
Column forms, 55
Column reports, 61–62
Control menu, 6
Controls, 72–74
Copying fields, 25
Criteria: queries, 44–48
Customised
    forms, 73–77
    reports, 79–82

Data
    checking, 27
    editing, 27–31
    excluding, 35
    entry, 12, 22, 58
    selecting, 24–25
    types, 14
Database
    creation, 16–17
    definition, 2–3
    management system, 4–5
    relational, 83–87, 88–91
    window, 7
Datasheet
    column order, 34
    column widths, 32
    formatting, 33
    fonts, 32
    printing, 35
    relational, 89
Datasheet view, 23
Default values: fields, 19
Deleting
    queries, 43

records, 30
tables, 13
Design view
    forms, 72
    reports, 79
    queries, 39
    tables, 12, 13
Dynasets, 41

Editing
    data, 27–31
    tables, 92
Entering data, 12, 22, 58
Excluding data, 35

Field(s), 8, 17
    list, 73, 92
    names, 9, 18
    properties, 19, 20
    size, 19
    types, 18, 20
Filters, 34
Find and replace, 28–29
Font, 32
Footers, 71, 78
Form components, 71
Form design view, 72
Form Wizard, 56, 58
Forms, 4, 54–59, 71–77
Forms: switchboard, 97–100

Grid, 75
Groups: controls, 74

Headers, 71, 78
Help, 9
Hiding fields: queries, 47

Joins between tables, 85

Labels: forms, 72
Lines, 81
Linking tables, 85
Logic in queries, 49–51
Lookup list, 23

Mailing label reports, 66–68
Mail merging, 68–70
Main menu, Access window, 6
Maximise button, 6

Menu bar, database window, 7
Minimize button, 6
Moving,
    control, 74
    fields, 25
    between records, 24
Multiple tables, 16

Null values, 93

Object list, database window, 7
Office Assistant, 7
Opening
    database, 6
    form, 56
    report, 62

Planning a database, 7–8
Primary key, 14–15
Print preview, 59, 64
Printing,
    forms, 59
    queries, 42
    records, 35
    reports, 65
    table design, 20–21
Properties: fields, 19–20

Queries, 4, 37–53
Queries
    closing, 42
    deleting, 43
    opening, 42
    printing, 42
    saving, 41
    viewing, 41
Query
    criteria, 44–48
    design view, 39
    design window, 39
    Wizard, 58

Record indicators, 24
Records, 8
Rectangles, 81

Relational databases, 83–91
Relationships, 83
Renaming
    fields in queries, 46
    tables, 13
Report components, 78
Report design view, 79
Report Wizards, 62–64
Reports, 5
Ruler, 75

Screen forms, 54–59
Selecting data, 24–25
Selecting records with filters, 34
Simple query wizard, 38
Single column forms, 55
single column reports, 62
Size: fields, 19
Sizing controls, 74
Skipping fields, 22
Spellchecker, 28
Status bar, Access window, 7
Summary query, 52
Switchboard forms, 97–100

Table design view, 12, 13
Table design window, 12
Tables, 4, 8, 10–15, 16–21
Tabular form, 56
Title bar, 6
Toolbar,
    Access window, 6
    Database window, 7
Toolbox, 73, 88

Undo, 23

Validation, 27

Wizards
    Documentor, 21
    Form, 56, 58
    Simple Query, 38
    Report, 62–64
    Table, 10